Searching Out Loud: Giving Voice to Independent Investigations

Searching Out Loud

Giving Voice to Independent Investigations

A Digital Media and Information Literacy Curriculum for
Reporters, Researchers, and Legal Professionals

UNIT THREE:

How to Source Information that Instructs

ISBN (978-1-7332554-2-4) print version
ISBN (978-1-7332554-4-8) e-book version

Some characters and events in this book are fictitious. Any similarity to real persons, living or dead, is coincidental and not intended by the author.

Promotion of the books, tools, applications, and creative works of...
 Romantic Deception by Dr. Sally Caldwell and Darlene E. Adams
 Finding Birthdays and Related Persons in One Step by Stephen P. Morse
 SurfWax search engine by Tom Holt
 Gigablast search engine by Matt Wells
 L-Soft and LISTSERV® trademark by L-Soft International, Inc.
 SearchEngineLand by ThirdDoorMedia.com
 WorldCat image and trademark by OCLC.org
 BRB Public Records by BRB Publications, LLC

Reprinted by permission.

Book Design by Davin Pasek and Emma Koramshahi of Paradise Copies
All photographs by the author unless otherwise credited.

Printed and bound in USA
First Printing September 2019

Published by The Society of Useful Information
4 French Street
Hadley, MA 01035

Visit www.searchingoutloud.org

For Patty, who taught me the root of all source knowledge:
Enduring gratitude

"I was gratified to be able to answer promptly, and I did. I said I didn't know."

— **Mark Twain**

"The most courageous act is still to think for yourself. Aloud."

— **Coco Chanel**

"No provider or user of an interactive computer service shall be treated as the publisher or speaker of any information provided by another information content provider."

— **Communications Decency Act, Section 230**

SEARCHING OUT LOUD
GIVING VOICE TO INDEPENDENT INVESTIGATIONS

CURRICULUM GUIDE

Here is the structure used for organizing the book along with the chapters for delivering the methods and skills for becoming Knowledge-ABLED through the Searching Out Loud digital literacy curriculum.

===

UNIT ONE:
How to Turn Information into Knowledge
Preparing:
How to Project Manage Virtual Investigations

===

UNIT ONE SUMMARY

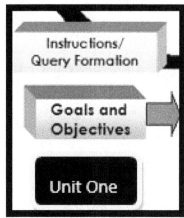

Our first section addresses search project management ("SPM"). SPM is based on the simple and often overlooked reality that being online costs a great deal; not in connect charges or even subscription fees but just by the shear amount of time we invest in searching, often with little to show for it.

Regardless of leaps in processing power, portability, and media convergence, there will remain a single problem reducible to two perennial questions: (1) what kinds of information are out there; and (2) how can what I'm looking for explain or even shape the decisions and actions I'll be making or revising?

SPM contains the discipline and focus that transcends technological change. In **Unit One** we apply SPM principles to recurring research assignments by setting out our information goals. To do this, we'll begin by defining what separates high from low quality information in pursuit of our project objectives. Then we'll decide on the appropriate research approach to our mission-specific projects. Finally, SPM gives us the focus to manage our search projects effectively so that the time and effort we invest is in line with the results we get online.

UNIT ONE SECTION STRUCTURE

1.1 Search Project Management: How do we assess what we want from our research sessions before we log into them

- a. How information becomes useful knowledge in pursuit of project goals and search targets

- b. An overview of the digital discovery process from initial exploration to knowledge mapping and informed decision-making

1.2 Search Logs: How do we document the successes and failures of our research according to the goals and objectives of our investigations

- ■ Pursuing search targets with discipline through selective documentation and action-based questions

1.3 Blindspots: What are some common traps and limitations that impede independent investigations and our effectiveness as researchers

- ■ Setting our information radar to gauge the awareness levels and blindspots of our search targets

1.4 Becoming Knowledge-ABLED: What is our role in bridging the divide between the communities we serve and the technologies that serve us as researchers

- a. What do search engines do and how do they work

- b. How search engines process information, where they get their processing, and how we can get them to do our bidding

Unit One Benefits

- ■ Learn and adopt SPM – A step-by-step process that helps us take control of Internet searches

- ■ Set goals, milestones, and resource limits for finding and applying pertinent information to our research projects

- ■ Build information radars that reveal where our search targets are spending their time and attention and where they're distracted or unaware (blindspots)

- ■ Identify the culprits that steal time from our virtual investigations so we can bypass them when they next arise

- ■ Figure in the time and expense we save by applying sound site selection practices

- ■ Calculate the value accrued in billing for our research services

Unit One Tables

- ■ The Knowledge Continuum – The challenge of using the web for research

- ■ Search Project Management steps and examples - Putting our cards on the table through search logs

- ■ Example search logs – Travel agents, caregivers, criminal investigators

- ■ Google search trade-offs for researchers - Working within search engine limitations

==

UNIT TWO:
How to Search for Information That Informs
Seeking:
Using Search in Virtual Investigations

==

Unit Two Summary

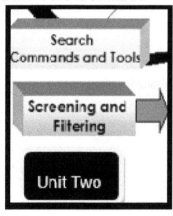

Unit Two is about tossing out the Driver's Ed instruction manual, getting in the car, and taking our established interests and new skills out for a test drive. **Unit Two** applies what we've learned about how search works to different engine and directory options. The goal is to conduct sophisticated, time-effective searches with a minimum of preparation and fees. Our priority is to focus on the best available tool and search strategy for the job at hand.

Having looked under the search engine hood in **Unit One**, we'll focus on tool selection, query formation, and refinement. We'll differentiate and select the right digital search and discovery tools, including visualization, cluster and NLP engines, as well as automated and human-filtered subject directories.

Next we start our meaningful exchanges with these tools by building effective queries. This means using the right search commands and word selection options for leveraging Internet resources, using correct syntax and semantics to express ourselves, and applying fact- and opinion-based guidelines to create productive outcomes.

Finally we draw on search operators, unique IDs, and pointers to either generalize or specify around the topics or our search targets – those events, policies, procedures, groups, or people in question. Our choices will depend not only on how but where we set our sights in the form of site selection.

Unit Two Section Structure

2.1 Query Formation: How to arrange, express, generalize, and specify our research questions

   a. What's a fair question and how to interview a search engine

   b. Conveying our intentions through syntax and search operators

   c. Refinements and corrections through term expansion and contraction

2.2 Semantics: What are the best terms for conducting research

   a. The role of informed word choice for building intentionality into search statements

   b. Applying unique IDs and verbatims to exact match and people searches

2.3 Tool Selection: What research tool to use and for which job

   a. Determining the right digital search and discovery tools for the questions we're raising, including visualization, cluster, metasearch and NLP engines

   b. Deciding on the right reference tools and recognized authorities in the fields we're searching including social media, portals, and subject directories

   c. Working with search engines, subject directories, or specialty databases when it's generalities, specifics, or somewhere in-between

2.4 Site Selection: Searching beyond search engines

   a. Where to do research and why size and location matters

   b. Determining the best starting point for the task at-hand

   c. Adjusting our approach to fit our resources

Unit Two Benefits

- Pose productive questions with a bias towards action

- Recognize appropriate search commands and word selection options for leveraging Internet resources

- Arrange and express effective search queries by using correct syntax and semantics

- Yield productive outcomes by applying fact- and opinion-based searches

- Generalize or specify around our topics and search targets by drawing on search operators, unique IDs, and pointers

- Overcome common pitfalls including familiar search detours, poor indexing, and character limits

- Reshape a misinformed question by redirecting our focus to more common problem sets and suggested searches

Unit Two Tables

- Defining what matters – The secret sauce of ordering search results through keywords, repetition, verbatims, and proximity

- Overcoming search limits – What we need to teach the search engine that it can't possibly know

- The haystacks and icebergs framework – Learning cues for opinion and fact-based searches

- Dialogging with search results through SEO (search engine optimization), unique IDs and pointers

- Answers, not documents – Defining natural language search engines

- Overlay of engines and directories – Precision versus recall

==

UNIT THREE:
How to Source Information That Instructs
Sourcing:
How to Evaluate Information Quality

==

UNIT THREE SUMMARY

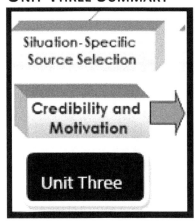

Unit Three focuses on acquiring source fluency and learning how to leverage those sources to improve the quality of the information you source virtually. The Unit starts by confronting the essential form of how information is delivered to us and the questions it inspires: Where is it located? What is it called? When was it done? Who did it? Why do I care? How do I find it again?

We can't possibly know everything and this is no less true for sourcing the world's knowledge. Committing an inventory of leading references and go-to experts on any subject is too daunting even for the reference librarians. Our goal is not to become librarians but to develop a skill called source fluency. Source fluency ensures that we're looking in the right place – even when we're a first-time visitor to unfamiliar topics. We'll set up a quality control process that not only reduces the search noise that clutters our screens. It also helps us to attract, analyze, and interpret the sources we need to fulfill our project objectives. We'll develop the quality of our findings on three levels: Search sets, websites, and individual pages (but only the ones worth opening)!

Unit Three is also devoted to unlocking the secrets, pitfalls and potentials of searching topic-focused Internet databases. Building on our **Unit Two** understanding of search engines (oceans) and subject directories (lakes), we'll dive into the information pond of more narrow and targeted specialty databases to uncover scarce and often overlooked information. OLP ("Oceans, Lakes, and Ponds") is the primary method for establishing: (1) source fluency, and (2) for determining *when* to pursue *what size* database in our virtual investigations.

UNIT THREE SECTION STRUCTURE

3.1 Information Types: How to integrate search findings into a useful form

    a. Surviving the search results page

    b. How information gets packaged in four dimensions – Entry-based, resource-based, view-based, and form-based

3.2 Source Fluency: How to cast our search nets for building source credibility and confidence

    a. Applying the concept of OLP ("Oceans, Lakes, and Ponds") to source the web

    b. Developing source fluency so we can apply sound sourcing methods no matter who's supplying the content

    c. How far to push and how deep to dig before drawing conclusions or reaching out to others

3.3 Quality Control: How to evaluate Information

    a. The three levels of quality control for skimming and assessing results sets, websites, and individual pages

    b. Determining when to use what source, including premium (fee-based) information and deep web (a.k.a. 'invisible web') sources

3.4 Managing Project Resources: How to price information's time and money dimensions

    a. Sizing up free versus fee – When it makes sense to use premium content and where to find it for minimal cost

    b. Using content groupings and specialty collections to narrow in on specifics or expand on topics

Unit Three Benefits

    ■ Use appropriate techniques to analyze, interpret, and attract the sources you need to fulfill search objectives

    ■ Regulate information quality – Focusing exclusively on sources worthy of our review

    ■ Conduct an editorial check to qualify web-based publications

    ■ Formulas to qualify resources, quantify our confidence in them, and avert the need to open individual pages

    ■ Recognize where the likely boundary lies between public and proprietary information

    ■ Know and apply the rules for uncovering overlooked information

    ■ Reap the benefits of grouping sources for justifying our source choices

    ■ Determine when the media becomes the story and not just the source of it

Unit Three Tables

- Quantity controls for testing the waters – Ratio of key indicators including the Google sniff test, and signal-to-noise formulas

- Link analysis for understanding the scope and reach of information providers

- The deep versus the shallow web – Why two Internets

- The media dietary chain – Recognizing source self-interest

- Using premium databases for climbing out of an information ditch

==

UNIT FOUR:
Sense-making:
Focusing on Information Context

==

Unit Four Summary

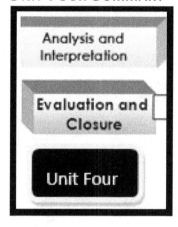

Unit Four has two principle thrusts: (1) Approaching research social networks as a researcher; and (2), engaging them as a member, including how to screen, join, attract, and communicate through virtual communities.

The slippery distinction between observer and participant is especially sensitive as we shift from the 'searching' to 'conversing'' phase of our research projects. This section focuses on ways to trail and gather background details on search targets that generate digital identities through their social media profiles, networks, and commentary.

The model we use for reading networks and acting on them is called provider conjugation. Like verb conjugation, this tool helps to establish the flow and context of how information travels and the perceptions it carries with it. We also apply it to ourselves as information providers in determining the perceptions we want to form about us. This includes the types of contacts we want to attract and build into our own networks – especially in reaching out to search targets that prove to be social media party animals, digital hermits, or somewhere in-between.

Unit Four Section Structure

4.1. Provider Conjugation: How to determine the motives of information providers in groups and as individuals

    a. Defining senders, recipients and audiences to understand the direction and speed that information travels

    b. Assessing the nature and trade-offs of individuals and groups as information sources

    c. Leveraging lateral thinking as a tool for conducting Internet research

4.2 Misinformation as an information source: How to use information rather than *be used* by it

    a. Taking the sniff test to grounded or unfounded suspicions

    b. Decoding the role that gatekeepers, watchdogs, and regulators play in scandal-making

    c. Picking up the scent of smoking guns – Red flag conditions for conflicts of interest

    d. Opinions online – How to know who is gaming the system or fabricating their credentials

4.3 The value of social information: Applying provider conjugation to social media

    a. Using social bookmarking to vet source experts

    b. Trapping information through RSS feeds to target new opportunities

    c. Building custom search applications to uncover key details

    d. Gaining media cachet through blogging and selective interviewing

    e. Joining a professional network, cultivating contacts

4.4 Search to Converse: How to get from reading about others to direct engagement

    a. The giant listening ear as a networking asset

    b. Bartering information among groups and individuals

Unit Four Benefits

- Background research the people you're going to meet – Deploy specialized search tools to gauge their web presence and digital identities

- Build a stable of advisers and referral networks for finding experts and second opinions

- Assess the differences between the way information is communicated informally through word-of-mouth and institutionally through groups

- Apply the Vectors of Integrity to determine the credibility of information providers and their own involvement in the issues they report

- Gauge the reputation of our search targets (it's not in the eye of the beholder)!

- Leverage social networking tools to raise our digital profile as an independent investigator

- Use alerts and notifications to stay on top of fluid and evolving situations

- Pick a blog theme that can be strengthened by our research

Unit Four Tables

- Social Networks – From soul searching to role seeking

- Using link analysis to determine social circles

- Common tagging concepts for breaking new ground and reclaiming past breakthroughs

- The Seven Vectors of Relationship Integrity – Using online communities to weigh objective and subjective-based experience

- Credibility Pyramid – The scale of public scrutiny

- Cultivating contacts – Defining boundaries and fail-safes

==

UNIT FIVE:
How to Present What We Learn in Teachable Ways
Presenting:
How to Connect What You Learn to Useful Outcomes

==

Unit Five Summary

We talk about opportunities when we use information. We think in terms of risk when others do so. **Unit Five** focuses not only on what we learn but how this works in relation to what others know and perceive. How can we as messengers assess the nerves we strike and the buttons we push in the research we're delivering?

The first four units focus on how to gather information and act on it. **Unit Five** is about how others will act on the research we deliver through social media and more formal, offline channels: The reports and presentations to peers, clients, and groups (our "audience"). How will our findings be interpreted and acted on? How we deliver them is every bit as important as the research itself.

Unit Five brings together the search project management steps, query formation, quality controls, source fluency and Information conjugation methods to deliver your research to the clients, colleagues, and communities we're supporting. These message receivers will clearly see how your informed use of web research tools and practices is bringing value, economy, and even closure to complex and resource-hungry investigations. We will then turn our attention to the report itself, coming to grips with the news we're delivering, the explanatory power of our analysis, and the changes we're proposing.

UNIT FIVE SECTION STRUCTURE

5.1 Message Delivery: How to Knowledge-ENABLE our colleagues, clients and community through our findings, analysis, reporting, and recommended actions

    a. Confirmable Outcomes – Reducing uncertainty, building consensus, and making reasonable assertions from complex and resource-hungry investigations

    b. Results Verification –- *Closing the loop* between the words and deeds as well as the facts and opinions documented through our search logs

5.2 Information Packaging: Bringing together the SPM structure, query formation, source fluency, and information conjugation to deliver winning reports

    a. Packaging the results – What they should contain, what to leave out, and how they should unfold as a learning narrative

    b. Assimilating search results, coverage patterns, and those elusive, missing pieces to draw meaningful comparisons and spotlight where the real story lies

5.3 Project Presentation: Conclusions, recommendations and next steps

    a. Drawing the line between independent investigators and the dependent actors we investigate

    b. Presenting clear and useful follow-up actions to clients and stakeholders without falling into decision-making traps

5.4 Post Investigation: Information-coping skills for self-managing our digital interactions

    a. Keeping the right doors open for continual discovery and professional growth

    b. Applying research disciplines to routines for managing our personal brands, virtual identities, and offline realities

Unit Five Benefits

- Differentiate deliberate from serendipitous discoveries
- Pinpoint conflicts of interest among our search targets
- Know where the bones are buried *before* you dig them up
- Legitimize the correct claims about conflicting facts and numbers
- Know and document the difference between confirmable facts and educated guesses
- Map research to primary intelligence and opportunities to barter information
- Assess the attention paid to our search topic and/or target and the broader issues they address

Unit Five Tables

- The certainty continuum for assessing the black and white (and gray)

- The candor of strangers and the corrupting influence of friendship

- The compromises to sound judgment posed by instant information

- Conversational icebreakers for breaking the case wide open

- Discussion maps for connecting the interests of our search targets to our project goals

===

UNIT SIX:
The Knowledge-ABLED Cook Book
Using Information:
A Recipe for Success

===

Unit Six Summary

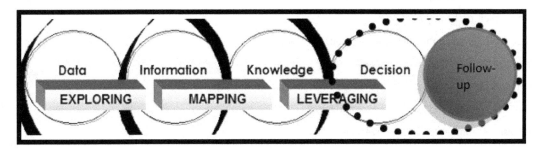

The book concludes with a Knowledge-ABLED use case based on the professional transformation of a commercial video producer to an educational media consultant. This use case guides us through the false starts and initial frustrations to the firmer footing and ultimate confidence-building that comes with being knowledge-ENABLED.

All relevant practices, frameworks, and search strategies in the case study are referenced to the specific units and chapters where they're introduced and demonstrated. For instance our use case subject entrepreneur plots out his research goals and supporting tasks through the Search Project Management model.

He applies the principles of site selection and Oceans, Lakes and Ponds to determine his sources, generate business leads, and build his understanding of the market and its growth potential. Finally he uses provider conjugation as a way of engaging the very same business contacts that first landed on his radar as search targets.

This journey is mapped out in three sections:

> **1. The Diagnosis** – We find out what makes our entrepreneur tick, how he's transitioning careers, and his challenges both as a researcher and a marketer.
>
> **2. The Search** – We apply the models and methods introduced in the first five units of the book to help scale the virtual research walls that were blocking the entrepreneur in the first section of **Unit Six**.
>
> **3. The Engagement** – We see the pay offs from the results of Part Two through our subject's ability to generate business leads, develop networking contacts, and narrow down to a selective and promising market niche.

UNIT SIX SECTION STRUCTURE

6.1 Introduction: Food for thought: you are what you eat

  a. Defining culinary metaphors and applying them to the research process, such as...

  b. Main ingredients, meal types, cuisines, courses and cooking methods

6.2 The Diagnosis: Assessing the goals and challenges of our case subject

  a. Initial intake – Coming to terms with internet confusion

  b. Better business targeting through site selection – Building credibility through reporting requirements

  c. Defining the boundaries – Scoping out the SPM to keep the project online and in line with our objectives

6.3 The Search: Matching the pursuit to the pay-offs

  a. The information ocean for generating and qualifying business leads

  b. The information lake for assessing market studies

  c. The information pond to get from trapping to acting on what we learn

  d. The book on RSS feed readers and their functions and benefits

6.4 The Engagement: The transition from searching to conversing

  a. Listening to markets – How to use RSS as a survey tool for mapping and confirming trends

  b. A review of the site selection techniques used to uncover the sources used in the case study

  c. The provider conjugation method for assessing the motives of information suppliers and how our subject is viewed by others as an information provider in his own right

Unit Six Benefits

  ■ Use term expansion to segment markets

  ■ Understand the situational specifics and efficiencies in the local search, clipping, and alerting functions of RSS readers

  ■ Connect individual experts to their key affiliations and then learn which groups are worth approaching

  ■ Generate feeds from news queries, news sites, and social media sources (event triggers)

  ■ Design a proactive follow-up to business leads triggered by daily events

<u>Unit Six Tables</u>

- Assembling the meal
- Gathering the research
- Mapping OLP to actions and outcomes
- Search Project Management Plan for our use case, (a.k.a. "George Reis Productions")

*While not part of the curriculum guide, **Unit Seven** lays out next steps for applying the perennial lessons of Searching Out Loud in the changing dynamics between information providers and tomorrow's Knowledge-ABLED investigators.*

UNIT THREE:

HOW TO SOURCE INFORMATION

THAT INSTRUCTS

Discovery at the Source

Source knowledge can be useful. Knowing who publishes what information and when can be a handy way to nail a popular reference question. The problem with source information is that it's limited to sources! The key is to understanding how the word gets around – why do individuals and groups want to play the role of publisher when the lead story is called: "What we know *(and want the rest of us to find out)."*

Unit Three focuses on our capacity to see the forest from the trees. This is how we analyze the emerging patterns from search results. This is how we connect the dots in social networks, group sources together, and decipher the prevailing themes, priorities, and popular notions that transcend any single website, news organization, or information provider.

Scientists describe these skills as fluid intelligence. These are the smarts that find meaning in confusion and solve problems, independent of what we knew prior to addressing them. Fluid is not reciting facts, skills people normally associate with brain power. **(Cascio, 2009[1])** In web investigations this ability is called **Source Fluency**. Source fluency is the set of Knowledge-ABLED skills we'll use to analyze, interpret, and attract the sources that inform our research objectives.

INFORMATION TYPES, QUALITY CONTROL, AND SOURCE FLUENCY

1. Information Types: First we'll focus on the delivery of search results. We'll learn how to channel an overload of details into the four basic ways that search results are pre-packaged in advance of our knowledge or knowing what to do with them. Breaking our results down by information types is the way we begin to impose our own order on the unstructured nature of unmediated search results.

2. Quality Control: Secondly, we'll apply a quality control formula that reduces the time it takes to go from searching to addressing our investigations. That means knowing where to invest our attention. The better we can document the quality of our sources, the more credible we become as analysts and investigators. To do this we'll consider three quality control levels for assessing results sets, websites, and individual pages:

> **1. Big Picture** – The equivalent of skimming the ocean so that the surface level details lead us to what's worth deepening our commitment.
>
> **2. Street Level** – We liken street level to one or several measured jumps into the information lake so that we can round up the best sites for the task at-hand.
>
> **3. Micro Level** – This is where the potential pay-off merits diving into the details at the source level.

3. Source Fluency: The nature and scope of our research questions changes with the wind. The sourcing of answers on the information ocean changes with the tide. How do we manage that level of uncertainty? It's not just answers. We need consistency and accountability from credible sources.

We must apply sound sourcing methods no matter who's demanding the answers or who's supplying the source materials. Source fluency enables us to bend, shape and mold the size and breadth of the web around the specific requirements for the mission at hand. Fluency is defined not as one but a series of techniques to analyze, interpret, and attract the sources we need to fulfill our search project objectives.

4. Managing Project Resources: Optimizing our research assets means knowing the extent of the commitment we're about to make. How recoverable will those costs be? Where can we side-step the time sinks that sandbag the most dedicated researcher? These sourcing issues all factor into cost.

Key to costing out a project is testing the eye-of-the-beholder: How much our clients value the work we provide them. Will that justify any out-of-pocket expenses and the extent of our due diligence efforts? Such cost/benefit calculations focus on...

- Determining when to use what source, including fee-based information and the deep web

- Sizing up free versus fee – When it makes sense to use premium content and where to find it for minimal cost, and

- Using content groupings and specialty collections to narrow in on specifics or expand on topics

Unit Three Learning Objectives

Let's take a glance back at the foundational settings from **Unit Two** that we'll be using as building blocks in **Unit Three**:

1. We explored how search engines can be fine-tuned to trap the particulars of fact-based investigations and increase the relevancy of opinion or concept-based searches.

2. We reviewed different filtering methods to help search technologies to interpret our intentions.

3. We presented several ways to anticipate the presentation of search results so that we can short-circuit the discovery process. That means presenting a complete analysis without needing to open individual pages to clarify *the why* in what we pull.

Unit Three Destination: Source Fluency

We can't possibly know everything. That's no less true for knowing who to go to. Committing an inventory of leading references and go-to experts on any subject is too daunting even for the most experienced reference librarians. Our goal is not to become librarians but to develop a critical Knowledge-ABLED skill we've just introduced above. **Source Fluency** ensures that we're looking in the right place. Even when we're a first-time visitor to unfamiliar topics. Source fluency has the open expectations of the beginner's mind. But it structures the discovery process according to (1) how search works, (2) the focus-bearing nature of investigations, and (3) the constraints of project deadlines.

Part of that discipline is a quality control process. It not only reduces the search noise that clutters our screens but also helps us to attract, analyze, and interpret the sources we need to fulfill our project objectives. We'll develop those quality controls on three levels: (1) Search sets, (2) Websites, and (3) Individual pages (but only the ones worth opening!)

In **Unit Three** we begin the interpretation process. Mainly, what do the results tell us about...

- The naturally selected sources (the ones we don't specify), and
- The ones we should call upon that would otherwise go unheeded in the investigation.

Unit Three focuses on acquiring source fluency and learning how to leverage those sources to improve the quality of the digital information we source. The unit starts by confronting the essential form of how information is delivered to us and the questions it inspires:

1. Where is it located?

2. What is it called?

3. When was it done?

4. Who did it?

5. Why do I care?

6. How do I find it again?

Unit Three is also devoted to unlocking the secrets, pitfalls, and potentials of searching topic-focused Internet databases. Building on our **Unit Two** understanding of search engines (oceans) and subject directories (lakes), we'll dive into the information pond. The pond provides more narrow and targeted specialty databases to uncover scarce and often overlooked information. OLP ("oceans, lakes, and ponds") is the primary method for determining when to pursue what size database in our web-based investigation.

In **Unit Three,** we take the refinements we explored through query formation and turn to the substance of what our searches turn up. We're not taking the search engine's word on what's news to us, or what's vital to our investigation. Sourcing information that instructs means our searches are informing our research objectives. An algorithm is no substitute for our own powers of sense-making: Our critical assessment of *why we got what we got* from our queries and how well this supports our goals for conducting them.

Effective information sourcing focuses on five Knowledge-ABLED practices for collecting and vetting web-based information providers:

1. **Information Types** – Understanding search results according to the form they're stored in as the first step in determining how well they suit our purpose and objectives.

2. **Source Fluency** – Knowing where to look for information without knowing what it is called.

3. **Site Selection** – Deciding how large a collection is appropriate for the questions we're posing.

4. **Quality Controls** – How to qualify our search results in the aggregate (by results sets instead of individual sites or pages).

5. **Managing Project Resources** – Costing out our projects so that our budgets can meet our delivery ambitions.

Unit Three Benefits

Upon completion of this unit, we should be able to understand and apply...

<u>**Information Types:**</u>

- *How do we break large chaotic sets of data down into manageable chunks of information that can be pieced together to inform our investigations?*
  This job is routinely performed for us by search engines designed to reward a pre-selected, self-interested, and opaque set of information sources.

- *How do we reduce those informants to the simple calculation of what's in it for them?*
  Only then can the merit of the information we're vetting rise above skepticism to qualify: (1) as evidence worth introducing to the investigations we conduct, and (2) the communities we serve.

<u>**Source Fluency:**</u>

- *How to source?*
  Use appropriate techniques to analyze, interpret, and attract the sources you need to fulfill search objectives.

- *How far to drill down?*
  Fluency helps us determine how far down to dig before reaching out to others, generalizing answers, and drawing conclusions.

- *How referenceable are the sources?*
  Deploy specialized search tools to gauge the web presence of target sources.

<u>**Site Selection:**</u>

- *How precise an answer do we need?*
  Pursue sources likely to produce definitive answers or cast an authoritative stature.

- *How relatable or connected is one source to the next? How does grouping our sources justifying our source choices?*
  Use the explanatory power of source groups to support client recommendations.

- *How original is the news we're getting?*
  Understand how providers package their information so we can integrate it into our client presentations.

Quality Control:

- *How do we access and evaluate sets, sites, and pages?*
  Review editorial checks to qualify information providers.

- *How can we be vested in the sources we select?*
  Use specific assessment criteria to qualify Internet resources and quantify our confidence in them.

- *How do we analyze large data sets in a consistent and expedient way?*
  Present a complete rendering of search results without needing to open individual pages.

Managing Project Resources:

- *When do we turn to fee-based sources?*
  Recognize where the likely boundary lies between public and proprietary information.

- *When do we go below radar for sources not indexed by commercial search media?*
  Know and apply the rules for uncovering overlooked information.

- *How do we trace the actual source?*
  Differentiate source inventory from news origination.

- *How do we understand the commercial incentives of our information providers?*
  Differentiate deliberate from serendipitous discoveries.

Definition: Source Fluency

Source fluency builds on source knowledge without becoming overly dependent on any one source. This is a core Knowledge-ABLED skill. Because of the web's dynamic and fluid nature, it's essential to pursue information sources with dexterity while remaining grounded in our research goals.

Searching Out Loud

SECTION 3:1 | Information Types —

How Do We Think About Information?

When designing a digital search strategy, it is important that we understand the range of available information on the Internet. What we are looking for varies greatly by situation, subject, time to discover, and urgency to know. However, *how we look* is critical, no matter what we're seeking. That's where the four information types kick in.

Back in **Unit One** we were introduced to two frameworks for conducting Internet research:

- **Search Project Management Forms:** Search logs systemically capture our search objectives in support of the project's underlying purpose. They provide a sequence-based structure for recording the approaches we take, the investigative tools we use, and the lessons drawn from our results.

- **Knowledge Awareness and Johari Window Frameworks**: Model for developing what and how our search targets see and interpret the world. These constructs are designed to solidify the often sketchy and ill-defined process of developing a person's frame of reference. They map to our awareness levels – specifically where we are most attentive and oblivious, a.k.a. our Knowledge-ABLED sides and our blindspots.

INTRODUCING INFORMATION TYPES

Information Types are another handy framework for transitioning search results into case evidence. In a world of complexity and shades of gray, information types suggest some welcome absolutes. Think of information types as our simple on/off switch. It's either black or white without sacrificing the subtleties of meaning, there for our powers of interpretation.

Where the **Search Log** is about documenting the discovery process, information types prepare us for a set of conditions we anticipate in the collection phase. Information types help us to organize our search results like no search engine can. That's because (1) it tracks the state that we find the information in, (2) its relatedness to our original intent, and (3) the purpose it serves for being provided in the first place.

Information types give us a vocabulary for anchoring our investigation in research terms that are well understood by researchers and most domain experts we're seeking to engage. Certainly they're a referenceable and transparent way to retrace the pathway that leads us to those experts. This is always a useful ice-breaker when we're trying to size-up how willing or capable someone is of leading us to that next step of discovery: The *why* aspect in our search project logs.

Finally, information types are a reliable and repeatable way to build on source knowledge without becoming overly dependent on any one source – the defining measure of source fluency.

The Damp Basement of Fruitless Searches

Remember the last time your spouse sent you down to the cellar to search? Only this time the search results included some kitchen utensil or dining room decoration? Wasn't there hiding in the corner? Maybe the search requester was right. It wasn't their fuzzy directions. It was that the search target here fell outside our abilities to recall, or even imagine.

Does this conjure up fruitless searches in storage areas that surrender shadows and mildew. But none of the mystery? If the thought of opening box-after-barren-box stresses you out, consider this: Imagine how most Internet users feel on an open-ended search of a conceptual and sketchy subject? It's not willful ignorance or even poor search etiquette where honest doubt succumbs to a stiff learning curve. We leave the water-logged search basement empty-handed.

The purpose of information types is to offer some solid and predictable outlines. Information types inform what the Knowledge-ABLED should expect to find before we ever formulate a query, select a tool, or manage a search project.

For example, are you document-centric? Think of your field of choice. Professions all adhere to their own scientific, medical, academic, regulatory, or legal reporting formats. A document-centric view is sound preparation to impose a task-based rigor on the discipline of integrating search results with professional objectives.

Defining Information Types

Information types encompass four categories commonly found in the most virtual investigations:

> **1. Entry Point** – How our search begins.
>
> **2. Resources** – The kinds of information sources that may turn up.
>
> **3. Point of View** – The subjective opinion of the information provider and motivations for making those views public.
>
> **4. Format** – How the information is archived or in what storage location.

How can we categorize and organize some common forms of information so they suggest next steps. These forms can help us predict what we will find in our searches, and further on within the sites worth our visiting.

Each of the four categories will include...

> ■ Between 3-4 subsets,
>
> ■ Shown as pairs of opposite characteristics, which
>
> ■ Play a role in assessing our project results.

The reason for the opposites is to create a range of outcomes or scale of possibilities. By opposites, we're not talking about the clashing of ideas or talking over each other in this age of hyper-partisanship. That comes in **Unit Four's** Vectors of Integrity. Rather, the opposing relationships in information types aren't political or psychological but specific to digital technology The range of these relationships traverse the many elements that impact our web-based investigations. Let's break this down into more concrete definitions and useful examples.

Entry Points

Where do we come in? Stage left? Perhaps before the last teardrop falls?

Navigating the web is not exactly an easy-on, easy off proposition. The road map can take us in one or several directions, or all of the above. We need to consider our point of entry in order to establish some gravity and orientation. What discussion are we eavesdropping on? When was the information first published? Just how public is this information to the communities it was designed to reach?

We also start with entry points because the questions we form and the search engines where we relate those curiosities are all familiar on-ramps for digital research. But it's more than search. We could be following a trail of blog posts. We could be browsing through a series of tags or bookmarks or Tumblr pages or Reddit articles. We could stumble on a site that speaks directly to our issues. Yet we can still be clueless about who, when, and why the information was ever published.

FIGURE 3.1: Listing out Points of Entry

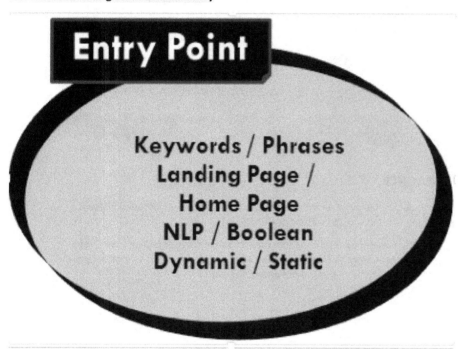

Entry points consist of:

■ **How we start out** – Are we relying on keywords only? Do we include phrases as search terms? Do we some of the advanced commands we introduced in **Unit Two**?

■ **Where we end up** – Are we being taken to a landing page, or the site root, or homepage listed in our search results?

■ **What search tool we use** – Do we trust a search engine to interpret our questions in plain English (Natural Language) or more traditional search commands (Boolean logic)?

FIGURE 3.2: Entry-based Information Types

Category	Information Types	Resource	Examples
Entry Point:	Keywords / Phrases	Keywords: Bag of words Phrases: Multiple consecutive word groupings surrounded by quotation marks	Lighting, floor plans, kitchens "interior design"
	Landing page / Home page	Landing page: Page extension creating to match query Home page: Root URL site	Froogle results Domain type is cut off
	NLP / Boolean	NLP: plain English questions Boolean: and, or, not statements	"What causes income gaps to widen?" Income and (disparity or inequity), not "class warfare"
	Dynamic / Static	Dynamic: Blogs Static: Site map	Page change alerts FAQs

PUTTING ENTRY POINTS INTO PRACTICE

Now let's put the theory into practice. Let's talk about the last time we expected clarity and hit a wall of confusion instead. What happens if we start out with high hopes of pay dirt and end up spinning our wheels?

By *spinning,* we're not talking about something ambiguous or half-promising that doesn't pan out. We're talking a total wipe-out with no recourse (and no resource). So how do we face down this wall of bricks? What are some common pitfalls or well-trod dead-ends that can be overcome by redirecting our searches down a more productive path?

First, let's unpack some of these familiar potholes in our search path:

1. **Disorientation** – This is the queasy factor. That knotting of our neck muscles when our searches are been kidnapped, blindfolded, and dropped under a bridge before sunrise. Most times, this is due to the co-opting of our intentions by link farms. These sites are the trolls lurking under that bridge. They exist for no other reason than to be landed on. Sometimes we land in a dust pile of confusion because a merchandiser has created a landing page customized to our location, click pattern, registration details, or designed to deliver audiences to inventories they're trying to move.

   CURE: Track our location back to the home page or root URL. Then we'll have a few breadcrumbs between the site owner and the hole we're climbing out from.

2. Ambiguous Terms – The leading cause of ambiguity is too few terms and too many nouns. Searches devoid of actions can compromise the outcomes we're testing or hypothesizing. That's a real problem because subjects and objects can't be clarified without predicates:

> "Google only returns exact matches for search terms ... so conjugating verbs, nouns, adjectives and adverbs catches a wider net of terms that people might search by." (**Stocking, Matsa, 2017**[2])

That rings as true in our ears as it does in the search bar. Information scientists call this 'disambiguation' – the process of matching word choice to user intention.

CURE: Disambiguation is a big word but our task is simple: Include actions that clarify the things we're looking for. This is the same problem as connecting causes and effects in web searches. We can't distinguish actors from their actions unless we apply the correct query formation. For instance, instead of searching on individual suspects in a criminal case, expressing this in **Word Algebra** terms:

*"(accused OR alleged) * (wrongdoing OR criminal)"*

3. 404 Errors – These are the hard stops and the dead-ends. 404s are the universal *lights out* sign that greets our untimely arrivals at defunct or malfunctioning sites. This is particularly vexing when we're retracing a path that we crossed days earlier, only to have the page pulled out from under our recent visits.

CURE: The easiest workaround is to recall the cache result. This is the most recent page record recorded by the search engine prior to changes on the live server or production environment. These disruptions are especially common on news sites. News stories may have a short shelf life, regardless of reader interest or longevity of the item being covered.

Definition: Cache

Cache results (pronounced "cash") is the imprint made by the crawler or search engine indexer. Cache results are the pages crawled and ultimately captured and processed by the search vendor. Cache results form the actual database that the search engine references before rendering the results page.

---

4. Over-precision – One way to price ourselves out of a productive search outcome is to become so consumed by our topics that they rob us of alternative ways for describing them. One student was fixated on the false claims of household cleaning products that he continually referred to 'deception in advertising' to the exclusion of its many variations. In these cases, we're not just looking for term expansion but topic headings that stretch our own categorical boundaries.

CURE: This is where subject directories are so powerful. They can generalize about specifics. They can overcome over-precision by augmenting the intention of the search without adding unnecessary details and unrelated tangents.

5. **Definitive Ranking** – There are two types of searchers: Those that make lists and everybody else. List-makers have a tendency to rely on rankings for prioritizing or comparing their *apples and oranges*. This is particularly common when needing to evaluate or recommend a product or even a problem-solving approach. As authoritative list is a common search goal because of the credibility it confers. The problem is that the more abstract the comparison or novel the topic, the likelier that the list-maker must act as their own de facto authority. It follows that source confidence comes first before determining the trust levels appropriate for web-based authorities and experts. Sourcing professional databases such as LinkedIn is one way to create better transparency between search rankings and subject experts.

CURE: The easiest way to swing the list-making momentum in our favor is to run searches peppered with the names of known competitors or choice ranges for handling the matter at-hand.

6. **Time Frames** – As a greater portion of our daily lives are spent on screens, the gap between when things happen in the physical and virtual world continues to narrow. Even so, it's not possible to reconcile traditional time series conventions like publication date and such anomalies as when that same article is time-stamped by the web server now containing the same file.

CURE: One of the major steps forward in terms of cataloging web content has been the emergence of blogs and social media for standardizing chronological sequence. The most trivial post on my Facebook wall comes with the time and day it was posted. This is a huge improvement over trying to approximate a date range in a publishing cycle by using 'months' and 'years' as key terms.

Definition: Disambiguation

> *Disambiguation is the process of matching word choice to user intention. This capability is especially challenging for search engines when users enter single search terms or incomplete information. GPS has emerged as a demonstrable way to contextualize user intentionality by the location from which they launch their searches, i.e. 'path' is not a metaphor for knowledge discovery but the physical address they're trying to locate on their phones.*

FIGURE 3.3: Disorientation on the Web

Pitfall	Challenge	Solution
Disorientation	Landing pages challenge our bearings: why did we land here?	Navigation to home page
Ambiguous terms	Context is not evident without further detail, e.g. "Convictions" – is this a number or a depth?	Quotes to anchor phrases, e.g. "how to sew"
404 error	Broken link based on discontinued sites or network interruptions	Use cache results that generate screen captures
Over-precision	We fixate on one hard fact or search target and generate zero "0" or limited search results	Unique IDs: From airline flights to UPC codes and tracking numbers
Definitive rankings	Exhaustive list in orderly ranking of all members worthy of mention	Inclusive groupings that expand on overlooked members or questions the status of others
Timeframes	The web is notorious for warping the chronological sequence of time and events	Focus on web media with a consistent time stamp such as social media postings

Before we move onto resources we should also consider some familiar pitfalls that we have little or no control over – mainly the inherent shortcomings of search technology.

Faults and Breakdowns

Let's plan our escape now that we've flipped on the lights in the chamber of search horrors. First we'll need to reconstruct how we got to this compromised state in the first place. Let's revisit some false assumptions we may carry in our search habits that sabotage our intentions as well as our outcomes.

Before we point the finger at ourselves for these roadblocks, we'll confront the source of our frustration. Let's take a hard look at what the most seasoned searcher cannot overcome: The inherent flaws and limitations of search tools. Here are some search engine detours. Two variations on query size form two such unwelcome points of entry:

> 1. **Indexing Size Counts** – Renowned web researcher and Google Hacker, Tara Calishain observes one of the overlooked but important limitations about search engines. Not only do they not index large portions of the web. They also skimp on the pages that they do crawl.
>
> Google has a particularly small cache (or file size) when it comes to indexing html pages or PDFs. That means that words not found on the surface of spidered websites are not retrieved in our search results. File sizes are no longer conform to rule standards which stood at 100K per HTML page in 2015.[3] This point was refuted with little fanfare or corroboration two years later.[4] Either way, if we anticipate searches that attract lengthy pages like directory listings or full text articles, skip Google.

One way to apply page size as a quality control is to check for it before clicking through to the site. For instance, if the page size is just 5-10K it may well be too small any index to find the details we're seeking. Some search tools like Bing are better, not only at increasing the page size but at displaying the depth of the page within its domain. This tells you how buried a page is from the site that spawns it, giving you a sense of a page's depth, or the overall site dimensions.

2. **Character Limits** — One trap door is recognizing how many terms we can use when we throw down the search dice. It's tempting to let Google intercept our thoughts when it shoots us suggestive phrases in mid-stream. But that limits our choices to the ones already carved out for us by the word index. It also means we're following the herd. This may work for shopping around and assessing search trends but it compromises our ability as researchers to tease out the details of our investigations.

Unlike results lists, queries can't go on forever. Google is constantly expanding the threshold for how many characters its algorithm can chew on but more open-ended arrangements pose their own risks and limitations. For example, what happens if we cut and paste a sample sentence from a useful response we get into the search box? How about an entire paragraph? We must assume that Google with imply the exclusive AND Boolean operator between every single term it processes. That kind of long-windedness is guaranteed to form a choke-hold around any web page other than that containing the source page itself. The limit as of this writing is thirty-two words per query[5].

Other search tools encourage long-winded queries that catch the subtleties inherent with complex topics. For these entry points, it helps to capture an abstract or summary and see how well the same themes and categories hold up beyond simple keyword matches.

TEACHING THE ENGINE HOW TO SEARCH US

Remember in **Unit One** when we talked about the inability of search engines to read our minds, let alone set our priorities and litmus tests? How do these shortcomings not defeat but actually liberate us from the confines of search technology?

For starters, the most brilliant query in the world won't produce a continuous parade of useful results. But it does keep our heads in the game. That's key to effectively rationalizing the response we get. In effect, reading *the minds* of search engines.

How does this work? More importantly, how do machine-made minds deviate from our own thinking?

Human logic is inferential. Ours is the mental domain of educated guesses and ballpark estimates. It is based on conditional, relative, or changing conditions. Search engine logic is well ... mechanical. It is binary. It can only be precise. It is 'yes' or 'no' but never both or conditional relative to an unknowable number of extenuating factors. The outcome is A or B. In fact it is a rather advanced machine that can conclude it has to be X or Y for Z to happen.

A human on the other hand can know that Z will happen regardless of X and Y based on familiarity, experience, intuition, or just plain commonsense.

Sounds Geek to Me

Establishing the right give and take with a search tool doesn't mean we have to become software programmers or native geek speakers. That said, interviews with computers are more productive if conducted on the computer's terms. This means using the tools and expressions that trigger useful information for our investigation. Not asking questions in plain English.

So what happens when our search results tell us one thing: The engine has no clue what we're looking for? One of the first prompts when we shoot blanks is to ask a series of inferential questions:

1. **Term Expansion** — The first level is of response is to widen your horizons with the following term expanders. C'mon, flex that instructor muscle within: Okay, sometimes it's called... what? What are some synonyms or like-minded terms? When was it last used in a sentence? Speak its name and listen for the response.

2. **Connections and Associations** — The next level is the connectors. These are the affiliations or relationships that are bonded to our search terms. Ready? Okay, it's related to ... what? What are the other topics, subjects and disciplines it touches? What's the strength of the association? Is it less abstract to think in terms of people? That's fine. Who writes about this? What are some common and reliable authors, experts and sources? As we saw in **Unit Two**, clustering engines offer some unexpected, but potentially useful outcomes.

3. **Results Lists** — The third level of coaxing in the education of a search engine is to look at the page characteristics of the content results: What's the size of our hit counts. (As we'll learn later on in **Unit Three**, it helps to know if we're fishing in an ocean, lake or pond). Do our terms appear in the titles or URLs or are they buried? What are the site domains? Are they commercial, foreign, non-profit, government or educational? We'll look at how to analyze results lists without needing to read a single result.

4. **Pages** — The final prompt is to dig into the details of the sites themselves. What are its unique properties? Is it original content or does it aggregate content from other sources? What is the nature and number of attributions or references to the site? How often is it updated and what's site traffic does it attract? Finally, we'll look at how to scan individual pages and sites to assess credibility and motivations. That's the quality of information based on the interests of those providing it.

RESOURCES

What do we mean when we refer to *resources*?

Resources refer to the value of the information we're accessing in terms of what it costs us in time, money, and quality. But those factors pail compared to their value to us as researchers, consultants, and investigators. What's our aim here? To demonstrate the pay-off to our colleagues and clients – that's at the root of our resourcefulness.

Perhaps the most important dynamic is not how dated an article is or how accessible. It's the line we can draw between external and internal. This is our perpetual status as an insider or outsider. It's a perspective that will serve us well as virtual investigators.

Those with membership credentials pass internal communications along whether they belong to is a company, school, church or peer group. External communications are *outward facing*. That's a marketing term that means how our group communicates with the outside world, especially group communications to non-members with a vested interest in how and what our group is doing. The marketing term for this group is *stakeholders*. Stakeholders span a broad cross-section of constituencies from customers to cousins, from parents to government regulators.

FIGURE 3.4: Listing out Types of Resources

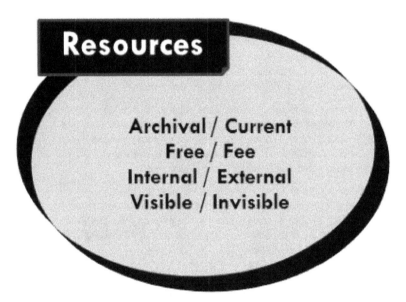

Resources are about...

■ **What they cost us** – Do the benefits outweigh the risks? We question this in terms of (1) recovering those costs through client fees, or (2) finding free sources that tend to disappear when the novelty wears off of non-revenue-producing resources.

■ **How far we need to dig for them** – What are the time commitments necessary for meaningful discovery? When do we pass the threshold for closing the due diligence loop on any number or nature of search targets?

■ **Point of origin** – Where do our discoveries come from? How does this impact the conclusions we draw, the probabilities we consider, and the recommended actions we confer?

FIGURE 3.5: Resource-based Information Types

Resources:	External / Internal
	Archival / Current
	Free / Fee
	Visible / Invisible

Here's a fuller accounting of the resources factor:

1. **External versus internal** – This is the connection between those providers and us as the recipients. Did it come from our employer or a group we belong to? Did we hear about it as a third party, removed from any personal affiliation with the newsmakers or those reporting it? The external versus internal perspective is especially useful for assessing how information providers source their own research. In other words, an insider's view from an outsider perspective.

2. **Archival versus current** – Time-wise resources can be archival, meaning they are pages stored in their original published form, or current to reflect the most recent update.

3. **Free versus fee** – In terms of cost, resources come in two familiar flavors. Either they're (1) free, devoid of passwords and shopping cart metaphors, or (2) fee-based, meaning we pay as we go or surrender our card numbers to the subscription renewal cycle. What information is in the public domain and what is either unavailable or proprietary, requiring an access fee? This black and white question is not always an open and shut proposition.

4. **Visible versus invisible** – Visible and invisible refers to what shows up on our results page and what does not, no matter how hard we look or deep we dig. The search results landing *below the radar* of common search engines is also referred to as **the Deep Web**. The abyss that falls between us and the Google search index.

FIGURE 3.6: Resource-based Subject Categories

Category	Information Types	Resource	Examples
Resources:	Archival / Current	Archived: Wayback Machine Current: Yahoo	Yahoo '96 Most e-mailed articles
	Free / Fee	Free: ERIC Fee: Highbeam Research	Lesson Plans Liberal Arts
	Authoritative / Dubious	Authoritative: Link analysis Dubious: Conspiracy sites	Wall Street Journal "Urban Legend" profile
	External / Internal	External: Newsgroups Internal: Communities of practice	Listservs Discussion boards
	Visible / Invisible	Visible: Google search engine Invisible: Infomine subject directory	Sponsored links Spider checking a dynamic database

PUTTING RESOURCES INTO PRACTICE

Before we move on, here are a few more pointers on cost.

It's odd. But no standard has emerged to determine when we should expect to pay for information and when we shouldn't. The closest indication is the simple question of whether we still want yesterday's news a month from now. The chances are if we do, it must carry more meaning than simply trying to stay informed about today's events. And we will have to pony up for it.

Not all sites function this way. Many trade magazines for instance keep their past issues available long past the typical shelf-life of a general circulation source like a newspaper or news magazine. Another way we can sometimes retrieve archival content free of charge is to use the cache version of an article as it appears in the index of the search engine we are using.

Perhaps the *kingpin of cache* is a resource called the **Wayback Machine**. It's a site that takes literal screen-shots of popular web pages and lists them according to the date they were indexed. Think *Wayback* for investigating any fraudulent business that used a website to substantiate what later became a baseless claim.

Viewpoints

At first glance, the term of viewpoints does not sound like a concrete example for grounding our expectations. We've all seen how one issue can create countless opinions, holding as strongly to the same view dismissed completely by an opposing side. How solid is that when we're trying to gain our footing? How reliable is that even for trying to describe our experience to the clients and colleagues we're attempting to support or influence?

Viewpoints, viewpoints and more shades of opinion: Who doesn't hold one? Who feels sure they know the most important ones to pursue? It's slippery going out there.

The purpose of an information type is to provide a guard rail to grab onto for describing, repeating, or avoiding any future investigations we conduct virtually. What about viewpoints? The term itself invites more questions than any working definitions, boundaries, or common ground for understanding the results we're reviewing, the sites we visit, or the databases we search.

Points of view consider...

- **How definitive or certain we can be** – Are we dealing with incontrovertible facts or softer, shiftier shades of opinion?

- **How far we need to dig for them** – Do they float to the surface of Google in plain view? Do we head for the deeper web that lies below the search engine radar?

- **Point of origin** – When and where does the content that catches our eye come from? Is it the original source or a conduit, a pass-through?

FIGURE 3.7: Listing out Viewpoints as Information Types

Point of View: Individual / Group

                                            Fact / Opinion

                                            Time-sensitive / Analytical

                                            Authoritative / Dubious

Here's a deeper dive into points of view:

1. **Individual versus group –** One of the most fundamental questions about the information we're screening is whether it represents one person's views or those of a group. That perspective is critical for determining the motives our sources hold for delivering the information now before us. Let's say for instance that we know a lot of folks have their hands in that process. What kind of group are we talking about? If the viewpoint is from an institutional perspective, is their core motive to maximize their profits, uphold the law, win a contest, or improve the communities they serve?

2. **Fact versus opinion –** How does fact and opinion play out on the web? If we're looking for exact dates, specific pricing, or precise wording our expectations should be for a rapid, *point blank* answer. Opinion-based assignments tend to run on and require more discipline to manage as search projects. A fact-based search with a hit or miss outcome works better on tight deadlines and finite sources. More conceptual search projects often feature both hits AND misses that defy brevity. We can get to our explanatory goals. But it's a conversation. Not an interrogation.

3. **Time-sensitive versus analytical –** Another dimension related to viewpoint is whether the information at hand is time-sensitive or analytical. What are our expectations around a cool, detached perspective when unplanned and sudden events occur? Should they be downgraded? Yes, perhaps so. At least until the preliminary reports are in, more likely after a full investigation is completed.

4. **Dubious versus authoritative –** The influence factor of resources can be hard to pin down. In the past, it was measured in circulation numbers for readers or TV households for viewers. Counts can still be generated for page views, file downloads, search rankings, subscribers (mostly unpaid), and dashboards of web analytics about our search behaviors. What's less certain are the beliefs that form in-between clicks. That's because the lines between content producers and consumers have blurred. So too is the once respectful distance between experts and laypersons has closed. The distinction between official news and unofficial speculation is also in doubt. We will address ways to restore some meaning to this important question when we focus on documenting credibility later in the Quality Control section of **Unit Three** and as we explore information context in **Unit Four**.

PUTTING VIEWPOINTS INTO PRACTICE

Category	Information Types	Resource	Examples
Point of View:	Institution / Individual	Institution: link:, related: Individual: Blogs	Corporate & educational sites Bloogz
	Commercial / Non-profit	Commercial: site.com Non-profit: site.org	Amazon (past purchases) Idealist.org
	Time-sensitive / Analytical	Time sensitive: news sites Analytical: in-depth investigations	Press release Christian Science Monitor
	Public / Proprietary	Public: Mandated disclosure Proprietary: Black market resale	Sex Offender Registry Personal bank statements
	Fact / Opinion	Fact: Times, places, specifics, absolutes Opinion: concepts, meanings, values, gray areas	Shipping schedules Caretaker strategy

Dubious Distinctions

By far the hardest definition to nail under Information Types is the slippery notion of information quality. The two extremes we present under Viewpoints is the degree of certainty we have in its quality. Are our resources authoritative or dubious? What's the determinant? One tangible way to think about quality is in legal terms. What will it cost the information provider in terms of their reputation and credibility if they get a story wrong? If it's a major publisher, the answer was once everything. Those costs have come down in a digital news climate. If it's an anonymous posting, a self-important blogger, or a source with a pre-set conclusion, the damage to one's credibility may be considerably less, even irrelevant to the desired outcome.

Facts, Opinions, and the Certainty of Outcomes

Before we move onto formats, here are a few more comments about facts versus opinions.

Fact-based searches are in a very real sense what people think of when they expect a certain outcome. A fixed objective requires a well-defined conclusion. It is a linear relationship between a stated cause and a clear effect. It is start-to-finish and the path is direct.

Fact-based questions fall into two categories: Transactional and informational. The transactional stuff can be summed up in one succinct keyword — shopping. However, the domain of facts extends beyond commercial transactions. There are archives of weather patterns. There are shipping manifestos that contain both immigrant populations and imported products. In fact, we could trace our ancestral routes through the slave trade when we return to a time that people and products were one in the same.

If there's a contract, a sale, a birth, or a milestone, most likely there are cyclical passages to mark...

- Its arrival,

- Gauge its reading, or

- Close the sales loop.

Feed a search engine a steady diet of digits and it will reveal patterns and cough-up the details. Better still, it will perform this tedious service with the same unfailing response regardless of the person asking or their motivations for doing so. To the human mind, this is the form of servitude machines were designed to assume in the Garden of Technological Eden. Unfailing reproductions of transactional trails and the paths they weave.

Informational questions are well within the reach of search technologies. In terms of milestones, what happens to us humans in our lifetimes is as finite as it is conclusive:

1. I went to this university and received that kind of degree.

2. You sat on that many boards and several involved working with the same management team that later hired you as the CEO of such-and-such.

3. She accesses hard-to-find audio files of her favorite songs through YouTube and searched Google yesterday for the easiest way to convert video streams to MP3 files.

In the above examples, there is little need to have personal contact or knowledge with these individuals in order to gather informational particulars. Personal histories all resonate from the addresses we've called home, to the scope of the networks we build in those communities. Even to the size of the debts we take out to finance those homes. Again, computers hold the memory cards so the informational stuff lies just below the transactional surface. The network effect of our movements and milestones tells us who we're likely to know, how we're likely to connect, and even how we size ourselves up vis-à-vis those comparable assets and peers in our social networks. That's the informational piece.

Then we wade into waters where no search engineer can approach from a position of strength. Soft, squishy, anecdotal experience. That's where opinion searches evolve from *concrete facts* to abstractions such as mental concepts, personal meanings, and non-financial values in our information-seeking information behaviors. Instead of needing a precise answer, we can start with a narrow objective and stem outward to include related associations and their implications. *(We'll see both approaches play out more fully when we explore the haystacks versus iceberg approach to sources later in this unit).*

Opinion searches fall into two camps: diagnostic and advisory. Both kinds of questions stretch the boundaries of information science because both types are complex in nature – for machines anyway. For instance, they require the resolution be based on a clear command of the actors and their actions.

The human brain is trained to handle this in our grammatical upbringings. We learn nouns and verbs. We can make tenses agree. We can tell a subject from a predicate and an object. There is little genius or novelty in bringing our sense-making to bear. It's what we humans do in processing information. We avoid repeating the same name for things when referring back to the same repeating *item*. We subtly avoid explicit meanings when an insinuation gives us the wiggle room to dismiss the threatened person as paranoid or too serious.

A diagnostic is information-gathering based on an eventual course of action formed from the findings gathered. An advisory is the recommended next steps: [We believe] this is the correct course of action based on the evidence gathered, the applicable options, and the probable outcomes.

Search on its own can't deliver on either count. But it can augment our ability to think more conceptually than computers. That's the essence of query formation. An informed view of syntax, semantics and operators may trick the search tool into doing our bidding for us. Ultimately, it's to help us ask better questions of the humans in our midst. That knowledge falls into levels of abstraction, experience, and understanding a synthetic intelligence is unlikely to touch in our lifetimes.

(c) Andrew Morris-Friedman

FORMAT

Finally, there's format. Format refers to the state we find the information in before we reassemble it to fit our own reporting structure or project goals.

Formats address...

- ■ **Completeness** – Do we want the full artifact or just the excerpt from our point of entry?

- ■ **Integration** – How much work is it to augment our reports with the content we capture from our web research? Does it come from a video? A flight reservation system? A spreadsheet? How do we embed these points of entry into our findings?

- ■ **Structure** – How well-defined are the containers that hold the information we seek? Are there tags that describe and generalize the broader meaning or aboutness of the pages we're surfing? Is the passage in question an explosion of words that come crashing down on us because of a random keyword match?

- ■ **Visibility** – How does structure play out based on what falls above or below the search engine radar? If we seek a highly structured outcome like a legal action or a shipping manifesto, is that our cue to google? Do we instead head straight for a specialty search or database resistant to search engine indexing?

FIGURE 3.8: Format-based Information Types

Format:	Structured and unstructured
	Metadata / Full record
	Indexed / Unstable
	Authoritative / Dubious

Here are the main factors in play when we consider format:

- ■ **Structured versus unstructured** — At its core, format is about packaging. How is the information organized? When we access professionally managed collections, we can choose the detail level we wish to delve: Prefer an abstract or summary? Do we insist on the full article or record? This choice is sometimes extended to free sites, sometimes not. Often pages containing free articles will vanish in lieu of a financial incentive to keep the archive available.

- **Metadata versus full record —** Then there's the basic question of whether we are looking for a number, an index, a database entry, a spreadsheet, a summary, or a full-blown narrative. Metadata are tags applied by information architects, librarians, and vested users that organize web content by categories and expressions we can browse, dispensing with queries and search engines. The meta-tags will steer us in the direction of specific collections, be they lists of licensees, articles on topics, or even directories of relevant websites. Once we click through to the source, we usually find whether the full article is viewable and downloadable.

- **Indexed versus unstable —** Where did we start out? Are we on a site or in a database? It's static or indexed if the page we're on was indexed by a search engine. We can re-engage it through the back button. The footing is less certain inside a database. If the page disappears once we leave it, we've been escorted there by a dynamic link. Not so stable.

PUTTING FORMAT INTO PRACTICE

Category	Information Types	Resource	Examples
Formats:	Metadata / Full record	Metadata: Gigablast	Lesson Plans
		Full record: 9-11 Report	Vivisimo
	Visible / Invisible	Case study: intext:"case study" site:edu	The Wharton School of Business
		Database entry: Town real estate assessments	Land parcel, physician performance history, etc.
	Indexed / Unstable	Indexed: Reference sources	About.com topics
		Unstable: aspx or cgi database results	Flights and reservations

Metadata versus Full Records

It may seem counterintuitive to the unwavering truth-seeker in us researchers. But most times it's the building blocks that get us where we need to go, not the building itself. Most times, we don't require the complete text to reinforce a supporting argument. We just need the recipe that can recreate our path back to the full recording source.

No single best search result is any match for a reliable set of keywords that are placed in the sensitive entry points of titles, addresses, anchors, and formats. That's the distinction between a keyword match and metadata. The former are what floats to the top of our search results. The latter is more powerful because it taps the plumbing that flushes out the Internet sewage. It's the metadata plumbing that produces pre-assembled and unique results. It's these granular findings that are tasked to our project priorities, emerging themes, and even reporting formats.

Stable versus Unstable

Anyone who makes a flight reservation on a travel site knows that we're not dealing with a permanent record or even a re-creatable event – unless we book the flight. The page assembled that shows available seats according to our timeframes, travel points, and price ranges is not a page at all but a snapshot. A placeholder frozen in time for a matter of minutes. It's what a programmer refers to as *a call* to a database: An on-the-fly assemblage of inventory gleaned from all the empty seats on all the potential itineraries that conform to our travel arrangements.

Come back to the same page five minutes later and that arrangement is scrambled because the price may have spiked. Our seats have been taken! That's what's referred to as a dynamic web search or unstable search outcome. How do we know when we're in a search environment that is not repeatable? Look for the lookup program that's been scripted into the URL of the web page. PHP? or CGI? for example at the end of a text-string tells us that this is not a static page but a dynamic one.It will expire during the same session unless we commit to the reservation.

Local Drive versus Network Drive

There's one more domain to tackle before we finish with the formatting aspect of information types. Let's focus for a minute on our own private universes that existed before cloud computing. They went by the name of the 'C:' or *hard drive* of our own MACs and PCs. What would happen if a total stranger looked at the way we organize our files? Would they have a clue what goes where or how we label and store our files? Is there a naming convention that we follow which they can too?

Chances are that all of us may be slightly confused about overlapping document titles and files that contain both copies, competing versions, and unique content buried towards the back. A certain effort is made to enforce electronic hygiene on a shared network. How would we leave a network drive clean and tidy, the way we would our bathroom sink?

For starters, we would give reasonable descriptions of a folder or file's contents based on precedent and order as much as on the whims of its author. There may also be efforts to embed document properties with common data fields such as a document's description, associated tasks, intended audiences, shelf-life, and/or entities, locations, and time-based information captured inside the file.

The larger point is this: Basic level of quality control are hard enough to come by when we're trying to clean up after ourselves – let alone what it's like to keep a whole houseful of databases in order. Figuring out the naming convention is a first step towards understanding the organizing principles of folders and files created in advance of our accessing them. In some instances ... way in advance.

SECTION 3:2 | Source Fluency —

How Should We Think About Documentation?

Unit Three is devoted to unlocking the secrets, pitfalls and potentials of searching business and reference-focused Internet databases. The goal is to conduct sophisticated, time-effective searches with a minimum of preparation (and fees).

So far, we've looked at internet research by getting a feel for orientation. Where am I when I come to that search results page, site destination, or highly ranked information source ... that turns out not all where I need to be!

Our discussion now moves onto where and how we can figure out our document needs. Not just the right length, formatting, and supporting detail but moving onto the sources we gather: Determining the credentials, credibility and very nature of the informants we intend to target. These determinants form the basis of our *source fluency*. Without it, we drift into two familiar and unproductive states:

1. **Source overload** — When have we reached overload? When we're more concerned about chasing down sources than the actual pay-offs: Finding evidence that will sway an argument, prompt a decision, or crack open a lead in our investigation.

2. **Source inventory** — Does it make sense to memorize the *top websites* by topic? Does it make sense to build a new list every time we approach one? That's called a *source inventory* and I don't recommend it. Here's why. Sources are dynamic. Archives are not. Websites launch, die, atrophy and refresh in a continual cycle of change. How to analyze, interpret, and attract the sources we need to fill our search objectives does not change very often. It means adopting and tweaking a few basic approaches that wear well — even improve, with continual practice.

LEARNING OBJECTIVES: SOURCE FLUENCY PAY-OFFS

Source fluency has numerous benefits. We will see how the size of our search pools affects the kinds of answers we get. We'll screen the results to avoid wasting time on redundant, bogus, or misleading information sources. Again, let's circle back to the first two units in order to understand where **Unit Three** is taking us:

1. **Filtering and Refining** — Better still, we will be able to package our reports to clients so they understand the "noise level" operating around the signal we're delivering. This will help us to educate them around the idea that *access* enjoys only a tenuous connection to *usefulness*. Our Knowledge-ABILITIES are helping them to acquire the right pieces, fitting them together, and shaping potential actions and outcomes demonstrated in our findings.

2. **Incentives and Motivations** — We will begin to see all the relevant facts and viewpoints gleaned so far by applying the SPM framework that we first introduced in **Unit One**. These perspectives will be guided by reviewing the incentives that information providers receive for (1) sharing what they know, and/or (2) rewarding the agendas they advance.

3. **Conclusions and Recommendations** — Where is this all going? Up ahead, we'll bring together the search project management steps, the refinement methods, the screening techniques, and the perspective-taking required to verify and resolve conflicting details. This clarity will inform our recommendations and prioritize follow-up actions.

Based on our ability to perform these activities, our clients will be able to see how our informed use of Internet research tools and practices is bringing value, economy, and even closure to a complex and resource-hungry investigation.

<u>Fluency as the Focus</u>

One of the biggest challenges to using the web for research isn't just about finding credible sources or verifiable facts. It's something even more basic and elusive. That's staying on track. Is our fundamental goal to check-out by resolving the reason we first checked in? If so, we need to get a grip around the distracting and fleeting nature of the web as a research medium. The chaotic nature of the web puts great claims not only on our attention. It's our ability to deal with ambiguous, open-ended questions raised by conflicting opinions from fleeting and sometimes untraceable sources.

Researching on the web is navigating through a maze of confusion. There's no avoiding it. Having our intentions garbled or ignored by search tools is a common predicament we face in doing digital research. Below we will find examples where searches are diverted by technical glitches, shortcomings, or commercial sites more intent on responding to their own business interests than our research questions.

<u>When Sources Undermine Answers</u>

Here's a bland and obvious roadblock to web sourcing: Internet information sources are confounding. But what's causing all the confusion?

- There are too many to keep track.

- We need to source them as well as the information they present to really *get* where they're coming from.

- The free ones disappear without warning. The ones we pay for usually ask for our credit cards before they vanish.

We need to adapt to the moving target of internet sources to be secure in our source knowledge. But few of us see source knowledge as the one-stop answer to a definitive question. Most of us rely on sources to settle scores and make decisions. Typically it's not the layperson but professionals who *fixate* on specific sources. That means they tend to see the information source as the prime, if not sole determinant for their search.

Promoting highly-regarded sources at the expense of most qualified answers isn't limited to lawyers, academics or journalists. It's a temptation for many of us mystified answer seekers. Limited topic knowledge to source awareness simplifies the problem: If it wasn't *in the Times,* it couldn't have been very important.

The other problem with keeping an open mind to sources is that by focusing on the 'what' we can sometimes lose sight of the 'why' behind our searches. For instance, maybe last spring we were looking for reviews of barbecues. This holiday season, we want one membership in the bacon of the month club for a loved one on our shopping list. Will our sources be the same?

Probably not.

Will the way we arrive at decisions be similar? Yes, indeed. We don't partake in *mission bacon* with an empty grease pan for catching the useless scraps from *mission barbecues.* Source fluency means never having to work from scratch. It means not having to reinvent what's already worked. We're not boxed in by self-limiting sources or answers to unique questions, conflicting answers, and constantly changing search conditions.

A Hands-off Approach

What would happen if we let the problem decide sources rather than the reverse? What would the result be if we wanted to encourage certain kinds of information without being too exclusive or prejudicial? What would happen if we could discourage the *fire hose effect* of too many sources – especially those whose self-interest does nothing to advance our own?

Below are some surefire ways for bumping into higher quality search results, without knowing a single source or expert:

FIGURE 3.9: Using Syntax and Semantics to Find Experts

Search Statement	Explanation
site:org OR site:edu OR site:gov	Self-interest of these sites not directly affected by the profit motive in many .com sites
(professor OR teacher OR author) bibliography	Authority or expert figures teamed with pointer term designed to yield more vetted references
"(how OR ways) to" "(search OR research) ** (web OR internet)" link:edu OR org	Connecting actions to outcomes within a set of non-commercial sources

THE HARSH GLARE OF FIXATIONS

Yes, it's possible to focus too much. Especially when our concentration returns to the same obsessive target. It's fine that we're engrossed in the work we do. But when the center of our attention is reduced to the first ten hits on Google, we tend to miss the larger picture. Myopic behavior works for heart surgeons and diamond cutters. But that kind of thinking can't adjust to the bumps and swerves of digital searching. On the web, flexibility is a more prized asset than single-mindedness. A successful search strategy is not about finding a seven letter word that means hello in one dialect and goodbye in another. In the impure and fast-moving world of the web, precise answers can work for formulas and facts, not for interpretative or abstract ones.

SITE SELECTION: THE CONCEPT OF PONDS, LAKES, AND OCEANS

We've considered all kinds of search technology, what different search tools do, and how to get search engines to understand our research needs. But what exactly are we searching at? Now it's time to point our search in the direction of where we're searching. Enter information-sized oceans, lakes and ponds, a metaphor for sources: Specifically, the number of them that may turn up in our searches.

Oceans, Lakes, and Ponds (or OLP) refer to the size of the database, collection, or index we're searching. The most sophisticated search tool is only as smart as the caliber of sources it collects and indexes. Conversely, the crudest of tools can uncover the most revealing detail if the database is exhaustive and the searcher knows how to search it.

The OLP concept uses the analogy of bodies of water to describe the size and scope of potential search areas. Another way of describing an ocean is a database of websites. That's what a search engine collects and organizes prior to our searching it. A lake, on the other hand, consists of websites that contain databases. Many of these databases cannot be searched through a public search engine like Google. They require us to be *in the lake* before we can actually jump in.

Defining Bodies of Content

So how do we define *what's what*? After all, there are no *ocean sources* any more than there are *pond subscriptions* or *lake-sized websites*. How do we apply these abstractions to actual destinations in our searches?

More importantly, when do we call upon an *ocean* of sites indexed by a search engine? When do we summon the *lake* of sites reviewed and categorized by a subject directory such as Wikipedia? When do we dispense with generalized bodies of information altogether? That's when we head straight for much smaller *pond* collections (that are much better organized!)

The Ocean/Lake/Pond concept uses the analogy of bodies of water to describe the size and scope of potential search areas:

1. **Oceans:** Oceans are a database of websites. That's what a search engine collects and organizes prior to our searching it.

2. **Lakes:** A lake is a website that contains databases. Many of these databases cannot be searched through a public search engine like Google and requires us to *jump in the lake* before we can actually search or browse them.

3. **Ponds:** Ponds are the databases themselves. You can google their existence, but you cannot search them until you're in the pond itself.

FIGURE 3.10: The OLP Framework

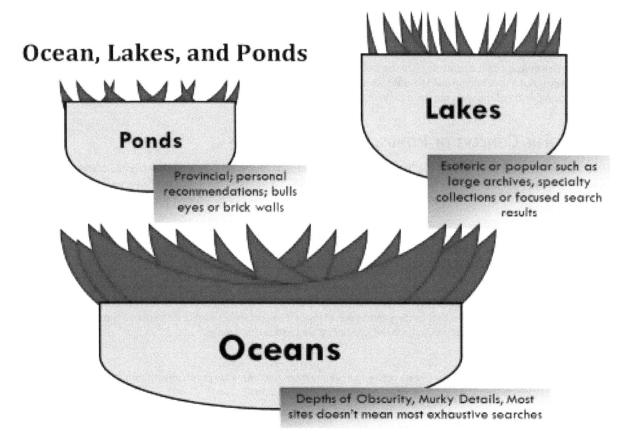

Working Samples

As we first experienced in **Unit Two**, Judy Hourihan's **Cookin' with Google** was a site that invited us to clean out our fridges. The answers were based on throwing a pot, pan, or casserole dish together. The questions consisted of selecting ingredients, then specifying the type of cuisine we wished to prepare. The customized *Cookin with Google* search demonstrated what it's like to search within your own personalized pond of information. This was a novel entry point for filtering content sources In a world that pre-dated social search.

A second example is **Worldcat**. Worldcat is an excellent human-filtered subject directory for producing peer-reviewed media and literature typically missed by the machine-enabled search engines and subject directories.

FIGURE 3.11: The Worldcat Subject Directory

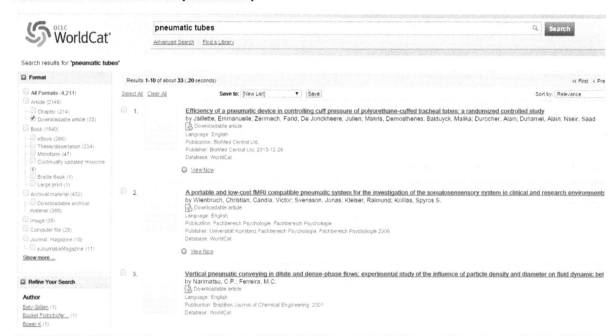

The Worldcat site will map tangible resources to the actual location (usually a university research library) where we can directly access the original source materials.

GETTING FROM AN OCEAN TO A POND

When semantics and syntax are working together ... well that's a beautiful thing. How do we get pulled into this magical mix? That's where we're zooming in on resources specific to our topic without sacrificing the comprehensiveness and detail we may need later on. When does our gratitude get tested? It's when the later on arrives. We know that information we're pursuing is *out there* – just not in the form we find it in.

As we'll learn this unit, there are large chunks of the web that land off the Google radar. In source fluency, we'll discover the Deep Web as an additional dimension to the ocean metaphor.[6] That's because the top search engines can only skim it. Plumbing the depths requires that we're fishing in a selective and *well-stocked* pond.

A pond refers to the countless databases that exist as gateways or starting points in Google but cannot be accessed directly without registering or at least accessing directly. A manageable number of similar sources are the essential difference between: (1) landing the big prey in a small pond, and (2) drowning in the open ocean, fishing for sites that never surface.

Here are some examples of how our **Unit Two** query formation tools figure into the sourcing process:

> 1. **Syntax** — This search features a long string of potential names for collections and archives referenced in the URL. Syntax enables us to gain access to databases whose contents evade the crawlers of common search engines like Google. Additional syntax further restricts the site domain to [.us site] – limiting the results to all state government-based web pages in the U.S.

2. **Semantics** — Including the term 'sex offender registry' was not a random decision. This popular phrase touches on such policy issues as the public's right to know and the sensitive area of privacy and constitutional freedoms. Strong media focus on the topic serves to inflame these passions by driving search traffic to the sites covering related stories.

3. **Pointers** — The word 'searchable' is a unique term that aptly describes the kind of outcome we're looking for: A database we can search. If we used the term 'search' in isolation ... chaos ensues.

<u>Putting OLP into Practice</u>

"This site comes up in every search. My client knows all this stuff already."

"I keep getting a certain view of events that are anything but certain."

"I was very disappointed, as I consider myself to be resourceful and fairly decent at digging up information/dirt in the past."

Dear tired, questioning, information seekers: I hear you. It's high time to file your frustrations under a mental placeholder called *getting from an ocean to a pond.* It's all rehash if we keep drinking from the information fire hose. While search engines have become better at shaping our user experience, that is largely a commercial undertaking. There are no algorithms to help investigators *shop for ideas* or *buy arguments.*

The trick is hooking up to a hydrant where we control the nozzle. Sometimes that means using syntax that refines our results better. Sometimes it's to use a different type of search that filters the results into discrete groupings. Sometimes it's better to predefine a list of sites and just focus on a narrow group of sources. As we saw in **Unit Two**, that's an availing feature of a CSE or 'custom search engine.'

FIGURE 3.12: Getting from Oceans to Ponds

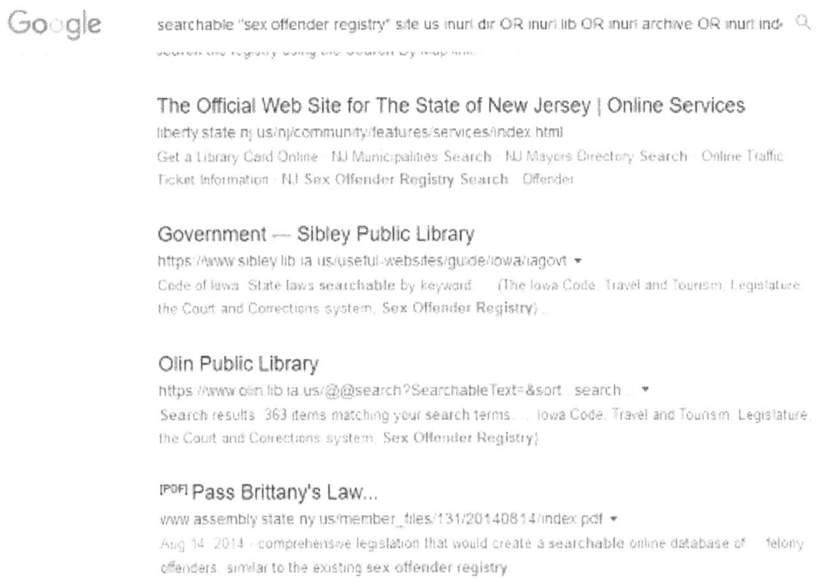

Google   searchable "sex offender registry" site us inurl dir OR inurl lib OR inurl archive OR inurl ind

The Official Web Site for The State of New Jersey | Online Services
liberty state nj us/nj/community/features/services/index.html
Get a Library Card Online · NJ Municipalities Search · NJ Mayors Directory Search · Online Traffic Ticket Information · NJ Sex Offender Registry Search · Offender

Government — Sibley Public Library
https://www.sibley lib ia us/useful-websites/guide/iowa/iagovt ▾
Code of Iowa: State laws searchable by keyword   (The Iowa Code, Travel and Tourism, Legislature, the Court and Corrections system, Sex Offender Registry)...

Olin Public Library
https://www.olin.lib ia us/@/@search?SearchableText=&sort search ▾
Search results: 363 items matching your search terms ... Iowa Code, Travel and Tourism, Legislature, the Court and Corrections system, Sex Offender Registry)

[PDF] **Pass Brittany's Law...**
www.assembly state ny us/member_files/131/20140814/index pdf ▾
Aug 14 2014 - comprehensive legislation that would create a searchable online database of   felony offenders similar to the existing sex offender registry

This ocean-to-pond expedition enlists the help of syntax, semantics, and pointers. Also note the total hit count falls below 3,000 for a target ("sex offender registry") that attracts over 800,000 pages.

The responsibility in running for the pond is that we really have to know what we want in advance of getting it. Investigative work has a long set of tasks that lend themselves to ponds. For instance, searching in a pond is implicit in every public records search. We will gladly surrender all the Google tricks we've learned because:

> 1. We're closing in on our target, and

> 2. It sure as well can't be found within Google.

Just as no one pretends to sourcing the water in a self-contained pond, so too, sane prospectors don't seek fortunes panning for gold in oceans. Are Massachusetts Doctors' malpractice records on Google? They're not. But we can use Google as a gateway to any number of public records sites where we get the real deal – primary evidence for our cases.

One well-established example for pond fishing is a patent search. Think of some common elements to dedicated resources like patents. Now think of some of the new syntax we've introduced. What happens when we include the following?

> *"searchable intitle:patents inurl:index (inurl:search OR inurl:dir OR inurl:directory OR inurl:database OR inurl:archive OR inurl:records)"*

In this example, the word *searchable* is a smart semantic choice since it exists exclusively to describe what we're trying to do. Use the word 'search' in isolation and it's like using the term 'environment' to describe global warming. (Good luck on finding the right 'search environment.') The other exclusions are that the term 'patents' exists in the title and 'index' describes the web page crawled by Google. Every other 'OR' is a rough attempt to land inside a pond that will help us find the granular bits we need to build our case.

Site Selection Factors

So which one is it going to be? Do we wait to book our tickets on an ocean liner like the next guy or do we attempt a soft canon ball off a rickety bridge into the creek? Can we hope to hit pay dirt (and not our shins and knuckles against some protruding rocks and branches?)

That process is called 'site selection.' Where do we cast our fishing lines for the prized catch? Factors that can affect which site (pond, lake or ocean) to start the expedition include the following:

> 1. Knowledge (expert) and ignorance (novice)

> 2. Facts and opinions

> 3. Time and expense

> 4. Simple questions, convoluted answers

Each pair of factors exists on a continuum. Determining where we are on each continuum is essential to developing a time- and cost-effective search strategy.

A search engine contains an ocean of information. It is far more useful to a researcher who knows what selective part is worth searching in than a novice with little exposure to the topic or actions under consideration. A subject directory is a 'lake.' It is far smaller in scale than a search engine in terms of its index and the information it contains is much better documented. Often, that's through the work of human classifiers. Not a *bot* or web-crawler in the case of Google.

In our ocean/lake/pond model, the pond is for diving while the ocean is for *skimming*. This is a commentary on both the depth of oceans as the cause of our drowning in information, casing the ocean surface by seldom looking beyond the first results page. Pond diving means that we have defined our information needs clearly enough to contain them – typically to one or several databases that would otherwise constitute drops in the information ocean.

In any search expedition there exists a tension between the guesses we make on the volume or supply of information at-hand and the answers we receive on the demands we place – namely on being able to act on the information we're given.

It's one thing to divide the overall supply into oceans, lakes and ponds. It's quite another to map these to our project requirements and our expectations for meeting those requirements. What site selection does is create a framework for determining where we need to be in terms of (1) our mastery of the topic, and (2) how far along we are in exploring it. We'll look at those plot points from four common site selection perspectives:

1. Knowledge and ignorance

2. Facts and opinions

3. Time and expense

4. Dates and locations

Definition: Site Selection

Site Selection applies the filtering process of the Ocean, Lake and Pond Framework to determine the most authoritative content sources for site and not search-based investigations.

SITE SELECTION FACTORS: KNOWLEDGE AND IGNORANCE

The black holes in Figure 3.13 suggest a couple of potential blindspots and failsafes for experts and novices alike. For the novice, the black hole occurs when they are besieged by deep, often arcane information about an unfamiliar subject. They are out of their depth when they encounter a foreign species: A specialty database that's organized according to criteria or classifications they can't follow or define for themselves. For them, perhaps a subject directory or Wikipedia entry would be a safer haven to begin their explorations.

On the other hand, an expert risks being subjected to introductory or commonly held knowledge that they've long since mastered. For them, a directory that limits the outcomes to scholarly works or academic journals may prove more productive. Better yet, a topic-specific database might contain the specific evidence or records they need to validate a hunch, test a theory, or confirm that they hold a unique piece of unpublished information.

FIGURE 3.13: Determining site selection through subject knowledge and ignorance

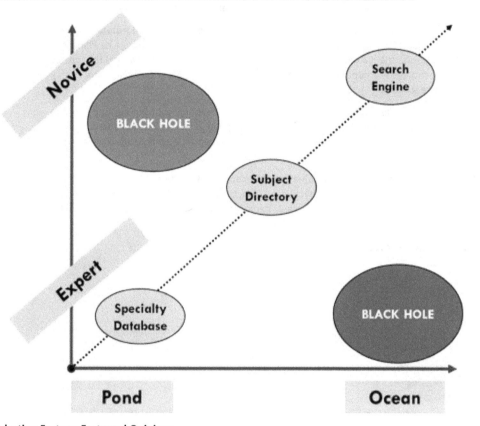

Site Selection Factors: Facts and Opinions

How do we fit our information-seeking goals (those facts and opinions) to the correct size of information sources we need to address them?

Oceans are the place to go for 'fact-based' reference information. Lakes tend to be better environments for delving into gray areas like subject-driven and opinion-based information. This is the province of topics and perspective-gathering. Ponds are dedicated to single topics. What we lose in the comprehensiveness of our results, we get back in relevance to the task at-hand. In our example, this might be the safety record of our car or the efficacy of a medication, given its side-effects, or interaction with other treatments.

It helps to wade into lakes when we're looking at unfamiliar subjects. If we know what we want, the ocean gives us more options. Ponds take them away but hold out the highest return on our research if...

- Our answers are fact-based, and
- We limit our focus to events and people through public records in the public domain.

We must be able to recognize and target the search area correctly to perform time- and cost-effective searches.

Most of us are not complete newcomers to the subjects we search. We're not typically world-renowned experts on them either. In Figure 3.14 we anchor to a set of facts (the lighter box on the Y Axis). Then expand our knowledge by filling in the most closely affiliated details (the darker box on the X Axis). We can straddle the line between the *known* and the *unknowns* we explored early in **Unit One**. The ideal strategy is grounded and expansive: *Grounded* in that it's rooted in some established facts or our familiarity with the subject.

Every investigator wants their fact-base to be *loaded and ready.* It contains numbers, locations, coordinates, and absolute values: The stark relief of times and distances calibrated to physical objects and mapped locations. But we also want to building from that strength. In other words, we expand our understanding by opening up to the complexities we invite in from the opinion side of our questions.

This is the analytical piece and from it enters human judgments, values, and perceptions. It is the less certain path. But remember this: It is less certain for all. The more insight and perspective we gain, the more credible our own opinion will become in helping to define the: (1) relative, (2) subjective, and (3) largely personal meanings that tug at the hearts of the folks we investigate.

FIGURE 3.14: Determining Site Selection through Facts and Opinions

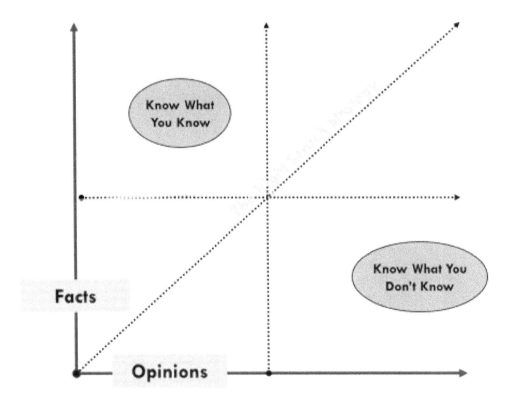

<u>Haystacks and Icebergs</u>

Here's an additional framework for understanding how facts and opinions play out in the way search engines process your query. The analogy of Haystacks and Icebergs helps to explain...

- How to select the right pool (ocean/lake/pond) in which to search

- Which tool to use for the type of search we want to perform

In this model, the haystack needles are the fact questions. The icebergs signify the opinion questions. Understanding how search engines interpret these different question types will help us to...

- Build better queries, and

- Receive results more aligned with our expectations and project requirements.

The needle in the haystack in Figure 3.15-3:16, top left, describes the exclusionary and exacting nature of fact-based questions. The priority here is to...

- Thread the needle,

- Strike the center of the bullseye, and

- Be vested in our use of source fluency.

Our confidence lies not only in the answers or where they came from but in the range of outcomes they suggest: We have a full accounting of the facts we need – whether they're...

- Unassailable or disputed, and

- On *our* side, or not.

FIGURE 3.15-3:16: Using Haystacks and Icebergs to Signify Precision and Recall — Two Opposing Web Investigation Methods

Haystacks
- Precision
- Facts and figures
- Specific details
- Implicit "AND"
- Unique IDs and pointers

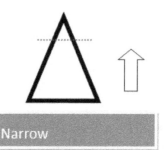

Narrow

Icebergs
- Recall
- Concepts and meanings
- Generalities and categories
- Implicit "OR"
- Opinions and influences

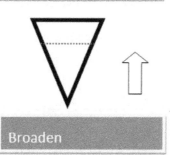

Broaden

The lower figure in 3:15-3.16 displays the iceberg (tip and all). The iceberg exemplifies the expansive and less definitive nature of opinion-based searches.

Searching Out Loud: Giving Voice to Independent Investigations | Marc Solomon

To the machine logic of a search tool, an opinion search is about keeping options open and entertaining possibilities:

> *I know for sure it's X but it could also be Y and Z or either Y or Z.*

Any level of uncertainty requires us to look more closely at: (1) competing versions of events, and (2) conflicting sources of opinion. To a search engine, this means an inclusionary outcome so long as that Boolean 'OR' command is present. The emphasis has turned from precision to recall: Being able to include as many potentially useful sources as possible.

SITE SELECTION FACTORS: TIME AND EXPENSE

In this book, we have begun to focus on how to be economizing with the amount of time we spend searching. We've begun to factor in the amount we spend on resources such as subscription-based information providers. We can now see the trade-offs between time and money. When it is justified to *call it quits* and consider offline pursuits of the answers we seek.

Most of us don't search for the sake of searching. We hunt for the thrill of closure, informing decisions, and settling scores – not for the pure *thrill of the chase.* If we reversed the query process and asked people about search engines, what might they say? Based on the widespread practice of unquestioning acceptance, I conclude most prefer their results not only fast and cheap. Ultimately, most would settle for free and instantaneous: The less need for interpretation, the better.

Just because most Internet access is either free or flat fee pricing, doesn't mean that fruitless searches don't carry their own costs. Generally speaking, research professionals are paid to find information quickly and budget their resources accordingly. The rest of us compensate for a lack of resources by hopping from site to site with often inconsistent and questionable results. Typically in a less efficient way. But a lack of resources doesn't necessarily mean a lack of resourcefulness. The trick is to yield productive outcomes with minimal effort. That's why we focused from the outset on documenting our SPM efforts with an emphasis on hitting walls, not home runs! So when do we play, when do we fold?

The upper right-hand quadrant in Figure 3.17 signifies searches that are too costly or time consuming. Generally this occurs when the researcher begins to sense their question cannot be answered by secondary or published sources. It requires firsthand or proprietary information to resolve.

FIGURE 3.17: Holding Down Costs and Time Sinks

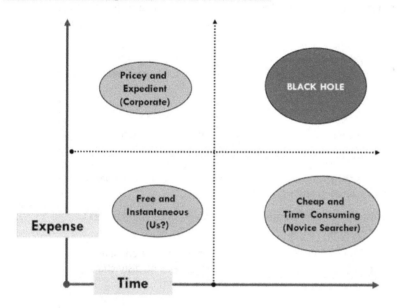

ESTIMATING OUR TIME COMMITMENTS

One way to begin measuring our effectiveness as researchers is to start timing how long it takes to get to *the bottom of things.* The path from ignorance to knowledge is rarely a straight line. Getting to the bottom implies not racing through *the middle* as-in running past...

- The unexpected, or

- Reasons for probing further.

In the search log that follows, we consider 5/10/15 minute intervals of search sessions. This diagnostic associates levels of awareness based on our time commitments. What happens when the same search is refined and repeated based on the addition of additional facts? New source knowledge as it materializes?

Consider the search log for a parking ticket dispute. Our motive is to avoid paying an unwarranted parking ticket. Our objective is proving the grounds for the ticket are baseless. Consider each milestone and whether the deepening time commitment is worth the effort:

1. **5 minutes:** Base level awareness of a common concern – *How to appeal a parking ticket in the neighborhood in question | Contact information for figureheads and bureaucrats*

2. **10 minutes:** Revisiting the issue from the violator's perspective – *Tips for fighting tickets that apply anywhere | Government sites that post parking regulations; individual motorists venting at un-posted rules; new crackdowns on illegal parking*

3. **15 minutes:** Corruption and suspicion in the administration of the process – *Hypocrisy in the papers | Corruption in the ranks, documented waiving of disputed tickets, etc.*

Site Selection Factors: Dates, Dates, Dates

Chronology – the art of plotting the sequential order of events – might as well be an ancient, outdated and lost science practiced by some dark, obscure research cult. We're sunk if we need to know what happened and when. Looking at a set of search results can be as edifying as trying to book a flight using a sun dial. Chronology is not spoken here.

It's hard to be sequential with a plain vanilla Google search. But we needn't let this limitation distract us from the end game: (1) A legal rationale for documenting the potential of wrongdoing, and (2) a timeline of questionable judgments that lead to legal trouble, even tragic consequences.

One suggestion is to shy away from the use of dates in general Google searches. There are ways to overcome the chronological shortcomings of most search engines that we'll get into when we begin focusing on important credibility factors like timeliness and ordering events in their true historic sequence. Not transactional dates like when a file gets uploaded to a site or when that site is rebranded by its host.

Getting in on the transactions

Another investigative instinct that serves us well in archival searches is to dig into the actual evidence, not to settle for media accounts of these same events. That's the stuff that's trivial at first, critical in hindsight, and completely disconnected from the crime until pieced together by the legal team. These are the logistics, event-planning, and operational details that are really on trial here. That's where the dates of filings and rulings trigger more accurate date ranges: Did this missed deadline, traffic infractions or court decision ever landed on the media's appointment calendar?

It's worth remembering that famous or infamous dates in history are search terms unto themselves: December 7th, 9/11, 2/23/03 for the Warwick Rhode Island night club fire use case that follows, etc.

In an investigation, the most significant aspect of dates is that they signify the sequential order of events in a criminal case. The problem on the web is that our timeline falls apart pretty quickly because general web search makes no distinction between when files are uploaded to a file server and when reality happens (events in the physical world).

However, as more reality moves to the web, that separation is becoming less clear. Even what constitutes 'an action' is changing. If a thought pops into a blogger's head and they share it without leaving their chair, is that reality? Maybe yes. Maybe not. But it's searchable all the same.

What we do know is the blog program runs on a markup language called XML. Unlike the HTML language that was with us in the web's formative stages, XML (and its offspring) embed the dates the files written to it are loaded automatically. That's why every blog entry is time-stamped. Sequential order has been restored as part of a publication calendar.

It's becoming easier to include dates in our searches when there is a direct connection between the time stamp on when a page is posted and the event it's depicting such as on news sites or blogs. Here are several examples for including date in our search:

FIGURE 3.18: Examples of Date Ranges in Web Searches circa Early 2000s

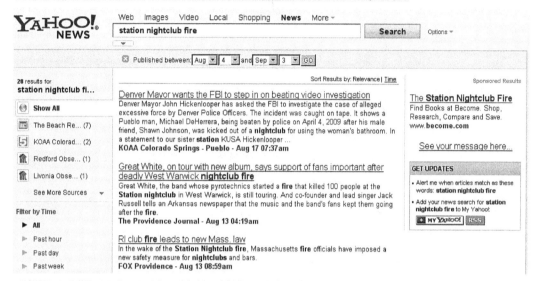

Note the date range option that pops up on Yahoo News searches. The same option does not suffice for general web searches or any collection where there is no linkage between an upload event and the chronology of an unfolding news story.

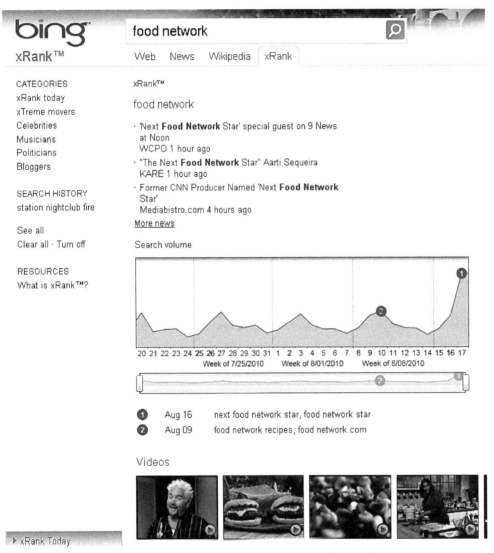

Time sequence metrics are applied here to popularly searched news items. Spikes in news coverage can be correlated to dramatic events or calendar cycles.

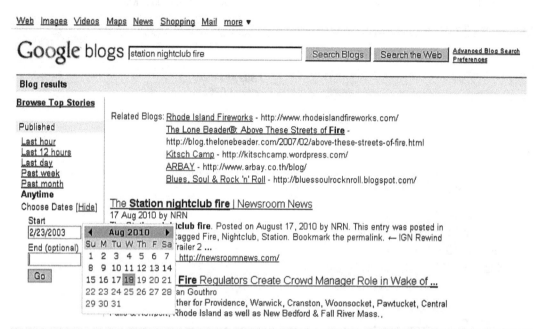

The time window option in Google blogs is a reminder that all XML-based content such as blogs, tweets, and RSS feeds are all ripe for timeframe searches. Google distanced itself from RSS with the 2013 discontinuation of Google Reader.[7]

Note that most of these date ranges are limited to a tight time window. An alternative is to gain access to fee-based subscription content through our local library or state library system. The best way to include meaningful date ranges is to search a commercial database like Infotrac and PowerSearch. They are free to search in my home state of Massachusetts:

https://libraries.state.ma.us

Archival Searches

Time is not only money but also memory. Records are routinely obliterated from view. When the site that reported compromising behavior about a school teacher in our district is removed from the story index, where do we turn?

Going back in time? That would be the waybackmachine.com site that features cache results of select websites and their periodic updates. The main site address is:

http://web.archive.org

It's intriguing to see how static and text-based it all appears when you return to the web through the Wayback Machine.

FIGURE 3.19: Examples of notable web archives

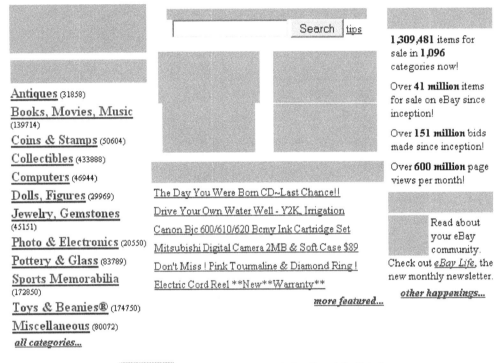

Antiques (31858)

Books, Movies, Music (139714)

Coins & Stamps (50604)

Collectibles (433888)

Computers (46944)

Dolls, Figures (29969)

Jewelry, Gemstones (45151)

Photo & Electronics (20550)

Pottery & Glass (83789)

Sports Memorabilia (172850)

Toys & Beanies® (174750)

Miscellaneous (80072)

all categories...

Search | tips

The Day You Were Born CD~Last Chance!!

Drive Your Own Water Well - Y2K, Irrigation

Canon Bjc 600/610/620 Bcmy Ink Cartridge Set

Mitsubishi Digital Camera 2MB & Soft Case $89

Don't Miss ! Pink Tourmaline & Diamond Ring !

Electric Cord Reel **New**Warranty**

more featured...

1,309,481 items for sale in 1,096 categories now!

Over 41 million items for sale on eBay since inception!

Over 151 million bids made since inception!

Over 600 million page views per month!

Read about your eBay community. Check out *eBay Life*, the new monthly newsletter.

other happenings...

About eBay | SafeHarbor | Bookmarks | eBay Store | Go Global!

Last updated: 01/16/99, 19:15:17 PST

Ebay in October, 1998

Yahoo! Deutschland   CLICK HERE TO VISIT THE STARS   **LOS ANGELES**   Weekly Picks

[   ] Search   Options

Yellow Pages - People Search - City Maps -- News Headlines - Stock Quotes - Sports Scores

- **Arts** - - *Humanities, Photography, Architecture, ...*

- **Business and Economy [Xtra!]** - - *Directory, Investments, Classifieds, ...*

- **Computers and Internet [Xtra!]** - - *Internet, WWW, Software, Multimedia, ...*

- **Education** - - *Universities, K-12, Courses, ...*

- **Entertainment [Xtra!]** - - *TV, Movies, Music, Magazines, ...*

- **Government** - - *Politics [Xtra!], Agencies, Law, Military, ...*

- **Health [Xtra!]** - - *Medicine, Drugs, Diseases, Fitness, ...*

- **News [Xtra!]** - - *World [Xtra!], Daily, Current Events, ...*

- **Recreation and Sports [Xtra!]** - - *Sports, Games, Travel, Autos, Outdoors, ...*

- **Reference** - - *Libraries, Dictionaries, Phone Numbers, ...*

- **Regional** - - *Countries, Regions, U.S. States, ...*

- **Science** - - *CS, Biology, Astronomy, Engineering, ...*

- **Social Science** - - *Anthropology, Sociology, Economics, ...*

- **Society and Culture** - - *People, Environment, Religion, ...*

Yahoo! New York - Yahoo! Shop - Yahooligans!

Yahoo in in October, 1996

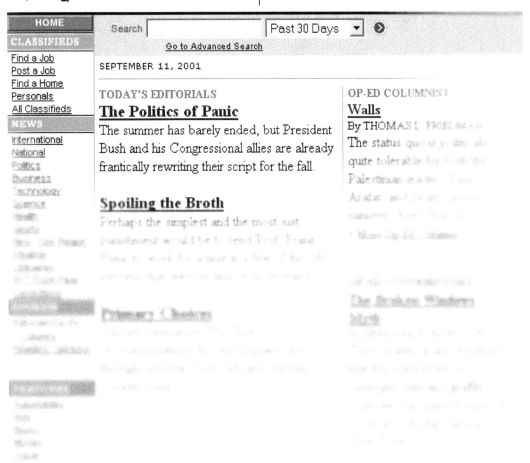

The New York Times Op-Ed section the morning of September 11, 2001

This tool is also helpful for tracking down fraudulent claims or controversial stories that get pulled when new facts come to light. But remember: This is not the definitive archival trail on all Internet sites we may want to track down in our investigations.

Site Selection Factors: Location, Location, Location

In addition to date, another elusive and often missing piece in web investigations is the notion of physical place in the virtual universe. It's one thing to check in on what weather to expect before we leave for work. It's quite another to document the weather conditions at the scene and time of a criminal act was committed. For that we have **Wunderground:**

FIGURE 3.20: The Weather as Evidential Exhibit

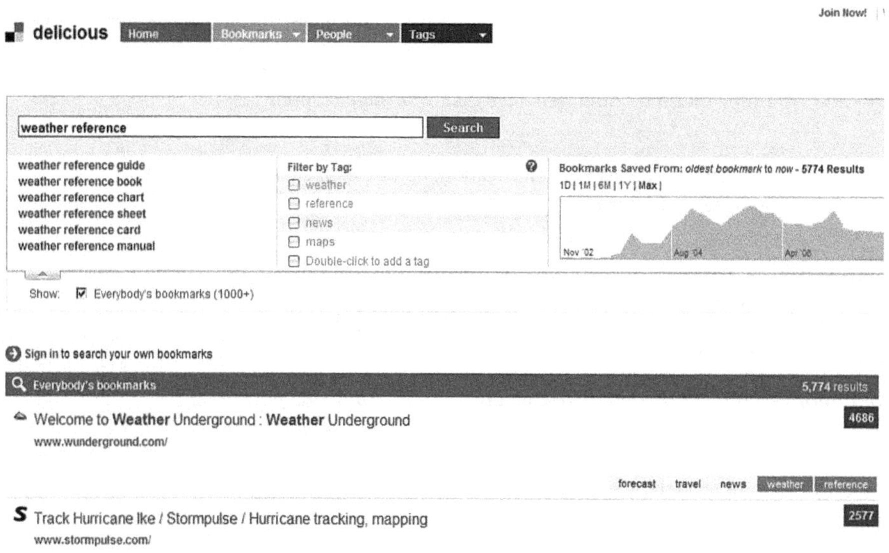

Here we use common labels from the once pre-eminent tagging engine called Delicious to identify sites endorsed by other Delicious members.

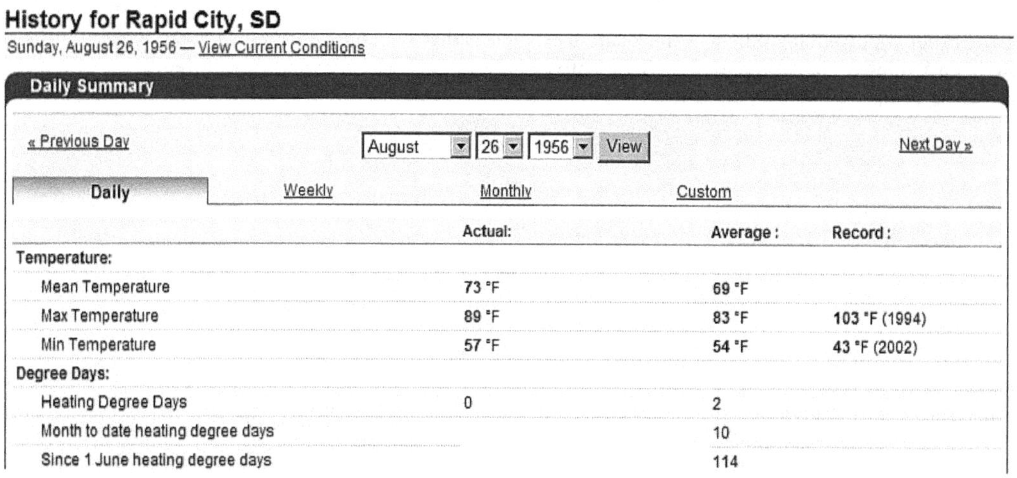

History for Rapid City, SD

Sunday, August 26, 1956 — View Current Conditions

Daily Summary

« Previous Day | August 26 1956 View | Next Day »

Daily | Weekly | Monthly | Custom

	Actual:	Average :	Record :
Temperature:			
Mean Temperature	73 °F	69 °F	
Max Temperature	89 °F	83 °F	103 °F (1994)
Min Temperature	57 °F	54 °F	43 °F (2002)
Degree Days:			
Heating Degree Days	0	2	
Month to date heating degree days		10	
Since 1 June heating degree days		114	

These are the spoils – micro details of a well-stocked pond like Wunderground!

Another example where location works is to search the geophysical proximity of bloggers to a potential crime scene in need of investigation. There's little mystery when it comes to mapping a local IP address to the actual residential locations of registered bloggers. While that may seem somewhat revealing, mapping search behaviors to our travel patterns has moved well past the invasive stages of profiling citizen users. *(More on big search and social media surveillance in **Unit Seven**).*

But what happens when we move beyond weather trivia and blogger tracking? Let's say we're looking to tweak our telescopic searches. Let's start with a routine example. What's a basic location question? Those have been reduced to simple GPS exercises:

> *"Where are the pizzerias near my local skating rink?"*

That's not where we're going here. What's a more complex one?

If we wanted to stump a natural search engine, we could determine whether it's worth attending our high school reunion with this:

> *"Where do my unrequited loves live now?Are they married? How well have their marriages turned out?"*

Either way, we end up nowhere in a hurry. Even in its most sinister forms of sophistication, no one expects web searches to lead us into the arms of confidantes or the beckoning doorsteps of informants.

From oceans and ponds to cities and streets

One way to factor in location is to return to the ocean to pond approach. To do this, we anchor ourselves in the LinkedIn directory, the leading social network of working professionals. Note the syntax that enables Google to focus on the one site. Then we add some semantics to approximate job title and expertise:

> *"site:www.linkedin.com "(group OR organization)(leader OR manager OR executive)(at OR from OR "part of"")*
> *("florida real estate law")*

Certainly there's *some* relevancy here. We can tighten it up though by balancing the semantics we've done with the compound search terms. We let the search breathe a little more with a few selected keywords. The real killer is to match job titles and expertise to actual cities in Florida. So we try this:

> *site:linkedin.com (realty OR "real estate") "(miami OR fort.*. OR tallahassee OR orlando OR tampa OR jacksonville OR st.*. OR west.*.) area" florida ~law ~investigations*

The second time's the charm. The other important ingredient in the location example is that searching ponds with ocean-sized search tools enables us to bypass some of the boundaries we bump into when we're looking up people on Facebook, LinkedIn, and other social networking sites

SITE SELECTION FACTORS: SIMPLE QUESTIONS, CONVOLUTED ANSWERS

The diagram below lays out the 'law of diminishing search returns.' This precept is an important project control check for making sure that we don't overstay our digital welcomes. Sometimes the best search strategy is to logoff, regroup, and fight another day. A respite from failsafes.

Generally speaking, the stiff-upper-lip approach is a non-starter for working through a research quandary. This describes a fixation on finding a particular person or fact without a backup plan: The benefit of an alternative outcome or substitute choice of search tools and strategies.

So, when should we quit? Generally speaking, it pays it reach for your second wind, if not second opinion, once we have the full regimen of search tools and resources under our belts. We've tried all our own tricks too within the scope of one hour. Ironically, the simpler the search, the more complex the outcome may prove to be. That's the typical dilemma of seeking a person with a fairly common first name and surname.

As anyone who ever tried to google the most popular high school chums will attest, asking a straightforward question can produce the most convoluted answers – if that search is unqualified or free of supporting identifiers.

FIGURE 3.21: The Law of Diminishing Search Returns

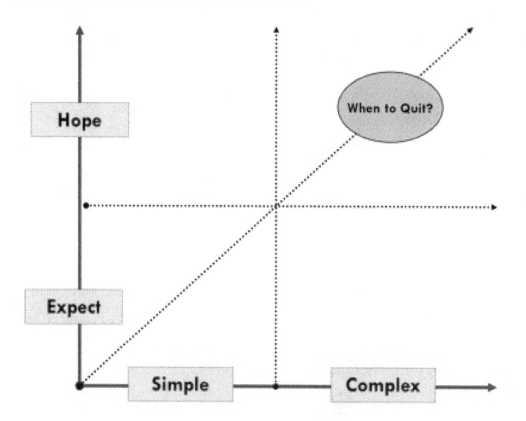

Facts v. Opinions

Let's break it down. Not by our objectives which here means finding the best sources. It's more basic than that. Our primary research goal is never about the size, number, or even quality of our sources. It's about getting our questions answered!

As we saw with the haystacks and icebergs model in figures 3.15-3.16, two dominant types of questions emerge: Fact-based questions and opinion-based questions. There's a good chance that our investigation includes elements of both.

We need to confirm or deny the recording of an event. We need to find out the road visibility on the date that a car accident occurred. But we also need to expand our questioning to include...

- Interpretations of what the recording means, or
- The eye witness testimony of the folks in proximity to the car wreck.

These factors are typical. Not only in terms of goal structure but in: (1) how they diverge in the types of questions they form, and (2) how this impacts both *how* and *where* we do the asking, a.k.a. site selection.

Here's that fact-based yes or no answer we must insist on:

We require the exact amount. We can't plan our day until we track the arrival of a parcel. Even when there are potentials for multiple conditions, we need to base our assumptions on a finite number of fixed conditions, i.e. reviewing case particulars like those that follow in Figures 3.22 and 23.

Opinion searches require *softer* answers that by definition are not *hard* facts. They evolve from concrete facts to abstractions such as concepts, meanings and non-financial values in our investigation. Instead of needing a precise answer, we start with a narrow objective and stem outward to include related associations and their implications.

The hard absolutes like weather conditions and prior driving record converge in our accident scenario. Then we move onto less certain variables like motives: Why the driver was in a hurry? Maybe their judgment was impaired in some other way: Poor signage, overgrown foliage, liabilities posed by the other drivers involved, etc.

Opinion-based searches are seeking subjective references for gathering perspectives on evidence that is by nature framed by experiences and associations – not definitive boundaries like times, dates, locations, or yes or no outcomes.

The best way to seek these less settled search targets is through a subject directory. A lake-sized directory attempts to show the multiple dimensions of a topic based on the diverse and sometimes clashing views of the people and organizations we are evaluating. With some sound sources and inferences, we can ascribe motives for their involvement or removal from our investigations.

FIGURE 3.22: Examples of Fact-based Questions (haystack model)

- **WHO:** Person, SSN

- **WHAT:** Company, Organization, Financial Index, Product Name, Facility, Weapon, Vehicle (Make, Model, Color, VIN, License Plate)

- **WHEN:** Date, Day, Holiday, Month, Year, Time, Time Period

- **WHERE:** Address, City, State, Country, Place (Region, Political, Geo-coordinates), Internet Address, Phone Number

- **HOW MUCH:** Currency, Measures

- **PATTERNS:** Rankings, Standards, SKUs ("stock keeping units"), Chemical Compounds, etc.

FIGURE 3.23: Examples of Opinion-based Questions (iceberg model)

- **CONCEPTS:** Unstructured Data, Good/Bad Actors, Spirituality

- **INFLUENCE:** Leadership, Role Models, Inspirations, Pastimes

- **TEMPERAMENT:** Principles, Tendencies, Character, Personality

- **PERCEPTION:** Awareness, Cultural Values, Socio-economic Status

- **SOCIAL NETWORK:** Affiliations, Events, Professional / Education Background

SECTION 3.3: | Quality Control —

How Do We Assess the Knowledge-ABLED Side of Websites?

In this section, we'll idle our search engines for a while to call attention to the review process for analyzing our results. As much as we can refine our results, tune our engines, and select from a wide variety of search tools, there is still a stack of stuff awaiting our inspection. That stack is bound to require more time than the hours in a day we have budgeted for searching out loud:

1. Anyone with a point to make can make one.

2. Anybody with an opening to post can circulate it for free – even if the opening is a fiction and it's only to test passing interest in it.

3. Any group with a shared interest can bond over it and invite others.

There are few risks or rules about using the web as you communications medium. From a research perspective, here's the bottom line: Most searchers can't process the pages they visit. The better you can document the quality of your sources, the more credible you become as an analyst and investigator.

We will consider the ingredients that go into determining the quality of our search results from a big picture perspective. That entails skimming results lists without needing to drill into individual pages. We will look from a street perspective which is to look at the ways to evaluate individual information providers. Finally, we will look from the microscopic level of quality control through page scanning: A technique used to evaluate individual pages and content providers.

WE ARE THE ONLY REGULATORS!

All investigators must remember that it is the responsibility of the information user – not the provider and not the search engine – to be accountable to the final arbiter of information quality (our research clients). Anyone can put up a web page about anything and give the First Amendment a run for its money!

Many pages are not kept up-to-date. Broken links are both a dead-end and giveaway that a site registration has lapsed. Equally bogus and more deceptive are expired site domains that have been resold to other controlling interests.

Regardless of ownership status, there is no government agency that handles web registrations. There is no central review board to determine the veracity, exactness, or reliability of statements, claims, or questions arising in or about web pages – especially allegations.

No quality controls mean that most sites are:

1. Not peer-reviewed or consumer vetted like a restaurant or a doctor

2. Less trustworthy than scholarly publications

3. Teeming with ads exploding with urgencies that underwrite and undermine our desire for commercial-free content

Does that mean we need to dismiss everything we see on screens? Does a lack of accountability mean the web is a questionable medium for conducting research? No. Not in the least.

What it does mean is the need for an approach that connects what's out there with meaningful standards to assess its legitimacy – namely *why* it's out there. To achieve this, we'll focus on three bottom line approaches for evaluating web content:

1. Through search engines (quantification of what's available)

2. Through subject directories (qualification of information providers), and

3. Through source conjugation (motivation for providing it).

But first, let's consider how shallow or deep we need to be in order to make these assessments. That means returning to our Oceans, Lakes, and Ponds framework in order to address the quality of what we're finding.

FIGURE 3.24: Key Issues Surrounding the Quality Control of Web Content

Quality Control
The only regulator is – Us!

Anyone can put up a Web page

About anything...and give the First Amendment a run for its money!

Many pages not kept up-to-date

Broken links are a dead-end/giveaway

No quality control

■Most sites not "peer-reviewed"

✓ Less trustworthy than scholarly publications

■No selection guidelines for search engines

✓ No commercial reward on "free information"

The Big Challenge:

Recognizing usefulness through qualification and quantification

There are three core ways (levels) to monitor search results.

The deeper the level, the higher our time commitment, as Figure 3.25 illustrates.

THE THREE LEVELS OF QUALITY CONTROL

The Bottom Line:

To realize that most searchers can't process the pages they visit. The better we can document the quality of our sources, the more effective we become as analysts and investigators.

FIGURE 3.25: The Three levels of Quality Control

Quality Control
Three levels of quality control
- Level 1 Big Picture

- Level 2 Street Level

- Level 3 Micro Level

Another way of looking at the three levels of quality control is to consider the following perspectives for focusing in on your research findings:

- **Level 1: Big Picture** – This is our first at-a-glance inkling of how close or distant we are from our Knowledge-ABLED destination. Our clues are in the form of titles, addresses and keywords. Since this is the entry level for casual surfers we need to pay particular attention to the *road most traveled*. It's one thing to learn all the tricks in the query formation toolbox. It's quite another to compare our superior SPM skills to the view of the web that our clients see. That cursory understanding is what floats to the top of the level one surface.

- **Level 2: Street Level** – We have now picked a handful of sites that show the most promise but we still need to vet the orientation of the site. That requires we understand what they're known for, who knows them, and what they do to shape the events they cover. From a social media perspective the street level needn't be so formal: what's the experience of clicking through? That's where we link site ownership, content generation, and keyword marketing to the editorial agendas of the sites in question.

- **Level 3: Microscopic Level** – The final quality check before a quote, fact, or important piece of evidence surfaces in our report. This phase runs closest to the basic tenets of journalistic tradition. This means the fact-checking once part and parcel to working in the newsroom. A reporter might be influenced by the beats they work and the informants they keep. But they are not the final arbiters of what sees print or *makes air*. Stories are corroborated, circumstances are confirmed, the sequential ordering of events is tested, and sources are named prior to publication.

Figure 3.26 lays out the key quality controls for assessing web-based research in order of granularity: results, sites, and pages:

FIGURE 3.26: Quality Controls by Assessment Level

Assessment Level	SPM Stage	Quality Control
Level 1: Results lists for analyzing keyword matches and influence of suggestion search and SEO campaigns	Review of search engine results lists	New-to-known Signal-to-noise Schedules Timeliness (date ranges) Locality (geographic ranges)
Level 2: Analysis for grouping pages according to common site characteristics	Screening pages by site root, (e.g., all pages share a common pattern such as .edu for education sites; blog in the URL for blogging sites)	Site ownership Site traffic Link popularity Link analysis Keyword analytics
Level 3: Page scans according to the motivations for publishing content, a.k.a. editorial agendas	Opening individual sites to vet content providers page-by-page	Tonality Story selection Content providers (message posters, authors, publishers, aggregators, etc.) Litigation Cache results (publication histories)

QUALITY AND QUANTITY CONTROLS

How do we read a set of search results? How do you make sense of countless web pages when we're not sure there's any definitive answer to our queries?

It's time to switch on our pattern-matching apparatus. We're going to go scouting for a few tell-tale signs:

> 1. Do we see a string of pages from the same site root or parent site?

> 2. Is the domain what we'd expect?

For instance, do we see...

> ■ Dotcoms light up our screens when our results have to do with purchases and financial transactions?

> ■ Dot.orgs and dot.edus if our questions are of a non-profit nature?

Is our intention to find and compare the differing requirements of states, localities, or other countries? This becomes apparent when our response includes dot.gov and sites hosted abroad.

Another important factor is whether our results come from a trickle or a warehouse of search pages. For instance, highly visible retailers and marquee corporations may have their entire catalogs inventoried on websites that span thousands of pages. A blog or personal page suggests the other extreme – even though the page may be hosted by an immensely sprawling host such as Facebook or Twitter.

The surest way to connect our query to search results still requires us to open the page and check for the prominent or fleeting appearance of your keywords. Are they close to the top of the page or buried in the terms and conditions?

The easiest way to trace this is to click on the cache or version of the page indexed on the search engine database. There are likely to be competing versions between the cache edition and what we see today on the production site – especially on frequently updated pages sites like those generated by news and entertainment sites.

Our first encounter with quality control starts in the familiar surroundings of the search result page. Here we'll introduce some new terms and tools like **content weight** and **new-to-known**.

Level I Quality Controls: Results List Analysis

A search results page is a listing of web page contents that our browser displays, which provide sufficient information to peruse without needing to open individual links.

There's no getting around the search results page. For search engines this is a universal billboard for their advertisers. For most of us (and I mean most people who find no joy in the act of searching) the priority is to escape level one ASAP. This escape is premised on two vital outcomes:

1. They needn't go past the first page

2. There are results to click on in the first place

But we can be certain of one thing whether we're in it for the research or the shopping. The faster we process a search result page the less time we'll flounder from site to useless site. A skilled deciphering can spell the difference between re-emerging with the jewels from a forgotten shipwreck – or drowning in the attempt.

The Google Truth

For the rest of us (I guess that leaves you and me) there's this remaining challenge: Result lists can determine information quality more than any single page, site, or ad that appears on them. That's because the first results page that assembles from commonly used keywords to frequently asked questions is our baseline. It tells us exactly what a layperson's view of a response looks like.

You and I are too curious, skeptical, and restless to accept the answers given. We're not going to succumb to suggestion search either. But in our haste to dig deeper, it is essential to reference this baseline. Especially when we are reporting the distinction between general awareness and the uncommon knowledge we deliver to our clients.

The other important bellwether here is to frame our results page experience in two words: What's new?

New-to-known

It might be time to move on if the deepest revelation is the dull surprise that the same erroneous facts we checked a week ago are now parroted by the Twitterpedia link farm. On the other hand if we're less familiar with our fresh subject then it's likely we're going to see foreign terms and strangers dotting the surface details. It may take 3-5 search result pages before we even begin to see a pattern emerge. This comparison of *new-to-known* is a helpful gauge for determining just how much Level One review is necessary in our search projects.

Content weight

Content weight was another helpful diagnostic that was discontinued in 2011. It told us the size of the web pages Google indexes. Generally speaking, the smaller the size, the better the fit of our search terms to the pages we're referencing. That's because longer pages are likelier to produce bogus results.

Size matters in other ways too. When trawling the ocean it's important to remember that we are not plumbing the depths. We are skipping across the crests of the waves.

That might not sound like a major readjustment when we're *submerged* in millions of search results. However an in-depth focus on specific people and events begs for the complete story when we're focusing on our results – not Google's advertisers!

FIGURE 3.27: Page Size Indicates Content Weight

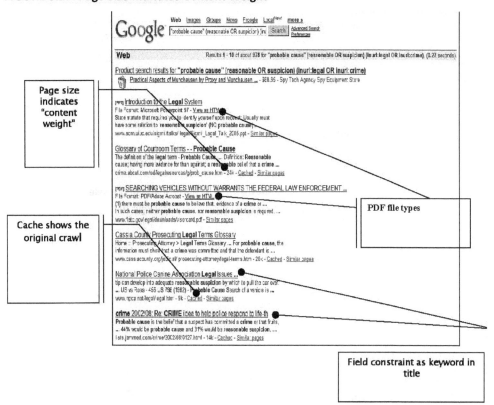

Cache Result

Cache results (pronounced "cash") is the imprint made by the crawler or search engine indexer. In an index as large as Google's it is a small imprint to be sure and it is rare to see a cache record exceed 100K per site. Even if that site runs not hundreds but thousands of pages just on its own! Cache is an important marker for establishing site revisions or wholesale changes such as when entire pages and/or sites are removed. It also best answers the question: "Why did I get what I got?." That's because we can see our keywords highlighted. This makes it easier to discern them in context and whether they're aligned with our learning objectives or *search intent*.

Site Root

Another useful tool to factor in is the concept we first addressed as an 'Entry Point' in the 'Information Type' section earlier in this unit. That's the notion of site roots in questioning whether the search engine is leading us to the main entrance or homepage of a website or to the side entrance. We'll be arriving unannounced if this is our first visit so we'll need to be expecting some disorientation. Even in above-board and well-documented sites.

File Format

One overlooked control factor in our favor is that we can contain your search results to file types whether they're stored as Microsoft Word Documents, Excel files, or PowerPoints, html pages, or PDFs. PDFs can be especially useful for web investigations because they hold a perception of higher credibility than a web page or even a Microsoft Word or PowerPoint presentation.

Why is that?

For starters, PDFs have long been the format of choice for editorial staff who wish to preserve the content and formatting of their written documentation in a read-only format. While it will become increasingly easier to convert PDFs to read/write formatting that sense of authorship and version control will remain a strong if not completely accurate property of PDF documentation.

This view is reinforced by the countless legal, regulatory, and academic papers that are saved as PDFs. If we're looking for government reports, public statistics, and other quantifiable evidence whether produced in a lab or a thesis study, chances are every table is preserved as a PDF. Something that appears "official" and peer-reviewed will often have the sheen of a PDF to set it apart from the more fluid formats used to post routine and daily changes to most websites.

ULTIMATE CONTROL OVER QUALITY CONTROLS

Okay, now. Let's put our terms up and post them where we can see 'em! It is reassuring to receive the stamp of our selected terms as top-of-mind appearances in the title fields of our search result pages. All search engines try to elevate the importance of our terms by literally pushing them to the top – not just of our lists but in the labels that describe the sites we attract.

As we saw in the 'Search Operators' discussion in the **Query Formation** section in **Unit Two**, it helps to be *general* in a *specific* way.

I know that sounds confusing but hear me out on this one!

One especially effective refinement strategy is to use the term expansion properties of the tilde with a word appearing in the title:

allintitle: ~strong ~opposition

This query will produce variations on the strength of the resistance whether our items include your original or like-minded terms. In other words a common expression is placed in: (1) a powerful context, and (2) an expansive scaling of that strength.

In the following Figure 3.28, we summarize these Level I elements when analyzing results lists:

- URL
- Domain/protocol
- Root / Cache
- File Formats

FIGURE 3.28: Level I Quality Controls

Quality Control	Example / Comments
URL – is this a group-based or personal page?	[~ or %] or users or members; sponsor links – *Who is at the controls? These are some telltale signs.*
Domain/Protocol – is this appropriate to our intention?	com, net, gov, state.us, uk, etc. – *What does the domain registration say about the credibility of the registrant?*
Site Root – are we on the parent site?	Generating .php or .aspx pages mean that we've stumble in the side entrance – *The key is connecting the landing page to the site root or homepage.*
Cache Result – is there keyword highlighting?	Changes between current and indexed versions – *Cache is helpful for documenting editorial changes between the production site and its archive as well as confirming why 'we got what we got.'*
File Format – is this a read only version?	docx, pptx, xlsx, pdf, mp3, htm, etc... – *What does the file format say about the quality of the information it contains?*

LEVEL I QUANTITY CONTROLS: RESULTS LIST ANALYSIS

As the title of this section implies, there is more than one way to read a results page. True, the more conventional read is to assess whether it's worth the leap from our questions to the responding site and page destinations. But another approach is to make the results pages the final destination.

The ability to read or interpret hit counts is a key pattern recognition skill and screening tool. It can help us to see the larger patterns that emerge so often in opinion-based and conceptual searches. Social scientists, authors, and most certainly marketers need to assess the bigger picture cultural trends before they can strike a nerve or tap into the popular imagination.

There are some major advantages to maintaining quantity control:

- Calculating hit counts (the number of results matching our queries) mean we can create better questions faster without the interruption of opening pages and needing to review individual sites.

- Establishing search metrics helps us to determine the likelihood of finding exact matches such as identifying unique targets, including people, facts, and locations, or isolating specific details.

- Quantity control is also important in terms of softer or less tangible targets such as testing awareness levels or the popularity of search targets. Looking at set result patterns is essential not only for correcting and perfecting search statements but also for distinguishing normal from exceptional levels of attention paid to our search topics and the topics we are targeting.

In the case below, however, we will stay quite literal. We will apply quantity controls to discern what mayhem is *real life* and what's been inspired by pure fantasy. In this case we will attempt to distinguish the actual crimes from entertainments.

TRUE LIFE CRIME: FACT "AND" FICTION

In the first instance we use syntax to go from an ocean to a pond. The contents of the pond are the bidding lots indexed on the auction site eBay. Here there are about 192,000 results containing an appearance of the term 'murder' But were real people involved more in commercial or criminal activity? Can we even assume reality when homicidal consequences hold so much sway over fans of horror films, pulp fiction, and whodunits?

Now the plot shifts. We add some semantics around escapism. Hark: The bottom drops out of our hit counts. We've reduced our result set to one-hundredth of its former size by focusing on non-fiction. We've eliminating movies, novels, games, comics, and murders committed by the pen and keyboard, not the weapons collected on the site of most crime scenes.

FIGURE 3.29: Level I Quantity Controls – Fiction and Reality

intitle:murder (manslaughter | homicide)   🔍

🔍 All   📰 News   🖼 Images   ▶ Videos   🔍 Shopping   ⋮ More   Settings   Tools

About 4,290,000 results (0.73 seconds)

In the first query, we're seeing 4.2 million hits for pages with murder in the title and the mentioning of either "manslaughter" or "homicide" on those same pages.

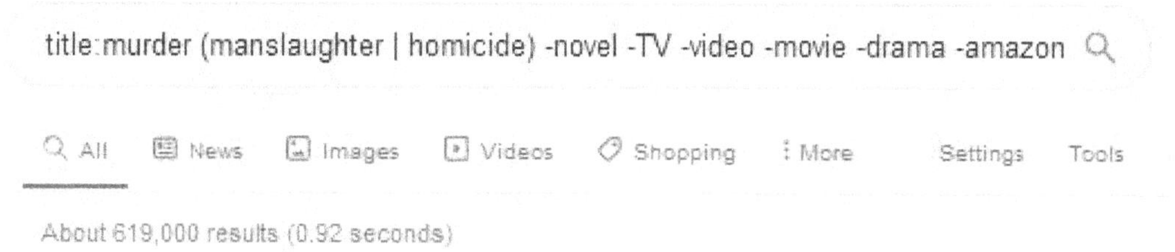

title:murder (manslaughter | homicide) -novel -TV -video -movie -drama -amazon 🔍

🔍 All   📰 News   🖼 Images   ▶ Videos   🔍 Shopping   ⋮ More   Settings   Tools

About 619,000 results (0.92 seconds)

How do we reduce the first result set by 85%? Remove murders told with the embellishments of fiction, that's how. Each negation operator eliminates another element of drama in the storytelling narrative. It's not only a text book case of information quality by subtraction. The massive hit reduction speaks to the realities of perception: What goes on between the readers' ears is likelier to populate a search index more readily than the evidence captured between the police barricades of a crime scene.

What does this tell us about human nature and how does this increase the quality of our investigation? Hands-down we've confirmed with numbers what we know in our hearts: Taking another person's life is a prolific part of our inner imaginings.It's a timeless way to tell stories, play out fantasies, and do some spectacular box office. From a Level One research perspective here are some other outcomes to ponder:

1. From four million down to six hundred thousand search results – what's a manageable basis to start the page level vetting process?

2. What do the page summaries for each hit say about *real life* events and how does that square with how people connect to them?

3. How does the fantasy aspect of the murder-mystery play into the escapist nature of dual personalities? Is that element a factor in the case of an individual we're investigating?

We can't read their minds but we can understand them better if say we don't know a gaming console from a roulette wheel and the gamer we're investigating seldom leaves their personal domain or what in pre-social media days the political columnist George Will referred to as the *electronic playground.*[8]

META SURVEILLANCE

Data mining is another way for applying quantity controls to web investigations. Data mining is the pattern recognition approach used in software programs that process enormous numbers of electronic records. The data miners are expected to detect the outliers or anomalies that diverge from the larger pattern. That's the rationale for using phone records to catch terrorists or to spy on persons of interest who would otherwise act under the cover of anonymity. Another is marketing. It's where advertisers and store merchants look for correlations from inputs like their ad spend and point-of-sale data to help influence what we buy based on our usage patterns.

Data mining is considered a best practice by companies who do business in the public arena. Their corporate relations and PR units routinely monitor newsgroups and neutralize incorrect information. These are rumor control functions that detect and understand rumors in their infancy and address them forthrightly on intranet sites:

1. Initiating early warning systems to detect possible sparks, (i.e. an upcoming labor negotiation).

2. Comparing the proportion of media coverage to differing crises.

3. What external forces should be part of your preparedness strategy? What reputation is worth protecting?

4. Scenarios for crisis management, including predetermined Q&A, approval procedures, crisis team contact information.

5. Best practice companies routinely monitor newsgroups and neutralize incorrect information – rumor control functions that detect and understand rumors in their infancy and address them forthrightly on intranet sites.

What innuendos creep into the questions posted to the crisis company spokesperson? How successfully is the crisis company in: (1) steering the discussion, and (2) responding positively to unfolding events? Is it being tarred and feathered by other vested, agenda-driven parties?

True Life Confidential: Data-mining for Medicinal Purposes

However, there's another emerging discipline around data-mining that's not related to espionage, retail marketing, or crisis communications. Those are the large data sets captured in the search logs of the digital giants (or what we came to know in 2012 as 'Big Data'). For them, what we ask has the potential to outweigh any conceivable service or product that can be sold over a web browser.

Google co-founder Sergey Brinn detailed the compelling nature of data mining search logs when he cited Google's two week jumpstart on the CDC ("Center for Disease Control") to confirm a flu epidemic. The evidence was based on a spike in the number of flu symptom-related keywords contained in Google searches done in areas where the outbreak was occurring. Google queries were a cheaper and more reliable data collection method than primary evidence-gathering such as checking drug store purchases of cold medications or tallying the number of flu diagnoses by local doctors.

In our case we never have to visit a doctor's office. We don't even have to open up another web page. Of course if we're getting the sniffles, it pays to proceed directly to Level Two Quality Controls.

LEVEL II QUALITY CONTROLS: SITE ANALYSIS

Up until now we've been using telescopes and field glasses just to grab a passing glance at the immensity and movement of the Web. We've now passed through Level I. We've used a set of quality and quantity controls and now we've cleared the Level I *Sniff Test*. That means we've reduced the noise and our signals are clear. Now we're clicking through on the hits we get.

We're also switching over from looking outward to inward. We're turning in our field glasses for the scrutiny of the microscope. We're descending to the entrance of Quality Control, Level II. Welcome to the world of website transparency: The way to maintain source quality at the site level.

Fit to Review

Traditional information literacy guidelines suggest that we verify the content we review. That's not only a tall order but an impractical task considering the dynamic and viral nature of non-vetted information. Remember how the only regulator is ultimately us? That's not just a bold statement about the web's potential to mislead investigators. It's also a cautionary reminder that suspicious accusations are often as untraceable as they are dubious.

A much more realistic goal is to determine what others say about our sources and who they are attempting to influence. We can sometimes estimate how well they are succeeding if we include quantity controls as well.

Rather than reading between every line, it's more productive to examine digitally-based evidence at the site — not at the quote, paragraph, or page level. It's possible to learn from second parties of fraudulent web sites. Another option is to scrutinize the publication history of works ascribed to specific authors. It's easier to hide in a discussion boards and social media site behind an alias or false identity. This shifts when content providers self-identify as authors because it is in their interest to maintain a consistency of brand. That's when we can begin to examine the biases and motivations of individuals that were formerly reserved for publishers and publications.

Aside from an editorial review, there are basic questions to be raised regardless of whether the provider is a soloist or group-based content provider:

1. How long has the site been running, how often does it refresh, and does that include follow-ups or corrections to priori art?

2. How much feedback and public commentary does it attract?

3. Is the information current? If so is it original or streamed from other sources?

<u>Level II Acid Test</u>

Contrary to the research traditions of print, a lack of objectivity on the web does not necessarily mean a source provides substandard information. To the contrary, a website at Level II may use unimpeachable data to the exclusion of less certain details that could raise more questions than answers. On the other hand, a preoccupation with inconclusive results may spark a rush to judgment when we need not be rushing or judging.

When analyzing content providers on the website level, it's critical to include the following Level II quality controls. The following quality control factors confer the intentions and partiality of content providers.

<u>Accuracy</u>

This is the former gold standard for what was once referred to as the journalistic objectivity of a free and independent press. The premise is based on the belief that a non-vested third party could present two sides of a dispute without becoming entangled in the debates they were reporting. That role as referee also included the ability to fact-check – specifically, to spot and sort through conflicts-of-interest between the debaters. A lot has changed in the news business since the advent of the web. *(A fuller assessment of the post social media impact on knowledge-ABLED practices is addressed in the **Unit Seven** Epilogue).*

But this much is clear regardless of one's stance on corporate self-interest, declining news budgets, and partisan clashes over what facts to check (and even how to check them):

Altered or forged evidence is rampant.

The opportunity to re-key or invent wholesale versions of news stories is easy to devise as such fabrications as plagiarized term papers or doctored news photos with photo-shopped faces inserted or missing from the original source materials. Plagiarism tools like Copyscape are effective for testing questionable assertions. Ocean-to-pond approaches that include myth debunking sites like **Snopes** (a.k.a. Urban Legends) are also useful for this purpose.

<u>Attributions</u>

In the print world a credible source would demonstrate the merit of its analytical rigor and source transparency with academic conventions such as bibliographic details, footnotes, and glossaries. Those markers still apply to academic and scientific journals. But the *fine print* of web-based content has been replaced in large part by hyperlinks, Facebook Walls, friend's lists, and even sponsored ads.

Site Ownership

Site ownership is a simple, effective way to assess commercial and other outside influences. This usually boils down to self-preservation or how the site manages to stay in business:

- Does the site accept advertising?

- If so what's the attraction and does it result in advertisers holding sway over the editorial?

- Are they prone to making claims? If so are they continually supported by the same sources?

Site owners and sources are another hotbed and often overlapping area of concern for establishing the legitimacy of content providers:

- Are there connections between quotable experts and sites they are quoted on?

- Are there recurring claims about the roles and responsibilities of an organization under investigation?

- Does that suggest a concealed agenda that would weaken the case being brought by the content provider?

Feeds and Streams

As anyone who's ever vetted information at Level II knows, it's rare that any single website is limited to a single information source. Even premiere news sites find it hard to resist the ease and economy of repackaging wire services and blog posts when an original news piece costs more to produce. That reduces our quality control issue to these simple questions for any single site in question:

1. How much of this stuff is theirs?

2. Where else does it appear?

3. How much of it reflects the inputs of vested outsiders who post on the site?

4. What's streamed in from other sources? For instance, are there RSS feeds from other publishers? Are these feeds further shaped to fit a particular audience or market niche?

LINK ANALYSIS

So what's a web researcher to do if bibliographies are slowly going the way of the do-do bird? While not a replacement for more established attributions, link analysis is vital. Link analysis traces the origin of accepted facts and quoted passages. An authoritative lake-sized database like Wikipedia insists on its contributors bundling the links from where they base their entries. Link analysis serves the dual social function for addressing a site's visibility and the type of visitors it attracts through back links, related, and similar pages. It also includes site ownership details we'll consider shortly with such a quality control resource called Alexa.[9]

In Level I questions such as 'bias', 'incompleteness', or a 'commercial' focus, our skepticism suggests that search results pages are skewed in favor of search vendor self-interest.

That doesn't mean search engine companies are inherently sleazy any more than one is nobler or publicly beneficial. As a researcher, it helps to play them off against each other: In other words bypassing the inherent weaknesses of one in favor of the collective strengths of the whole. That's one benefit of the metasearch capabilities we introduced in the 'Metasearch Engine' discussion in **Unit Two**. We really get to see the huge discrepancies between the entrenched, mainstays of web search.

Why is that? Aren't they all pretty much the same?

Actually they're not. Not only do results vary. But they also differ in the way they deliver results.

Quite a bit, in fact.

For example, Google is highly restrictive about what it will divulge about linking practices for fear that search engine marketers will try to skew its PageRank formula in favor of the sites they own – READ: Gaming the system. Because of that vulnerability, other search engines tend to be more open about which pages link to the sites we're evaluating. Thus, easier to conduct a meaningful link analysis. This is an important assessment for determining what an information source says about itself and how that contrasts to what outside parties have to say.

What does this have to do with site evaluations or quality control?

Generally speaking, the less commercial a website appears the more credible it may seem. But the potential for bias remains in play even when motivations are unclear. That's where a rounded knowledge is our best defense against our wholesale acceptance of 'the whole story' from any single source. A deeper understanding means an appreciation for the degree of completeness from each content provider. Link analysis also means independently verifying the sprawl of validations and potential sponsorships generated by the overall web presence of the site in question.

TRANSPARENCY AND SITE OWNERSHIP

Another approach for vetting websites is to focus on the ownership details of the site in question. **Alexa** is one example of a transparency tool that identifies mission through the site's 'About Us' statement, links, traffic patterns and site registration status. About Us statements are not only helpful for establishing a baseline awareness but can help distinguish the editorial tone, i.e. serious intent from humor.

Alexa ranks websites according to site visits, referring links, and connection speed. The site also connects a Whois lookup (site owner) as well as cache histories of the site over time (**Wayback Machine**). It also saves (or caches) our own search history and compiles that for creating a suggestion list of sites accrued by all site visitors who have entered the one in question.

In sum, Alexa provides a single reference tool for finding:

1. Site ownership

2. Reciprocal links that reference the site in question

3. Site popularity, including speed and site traffic (number of visitors)

4. Related sites in the form of other sites visited prior to this one

FIGURE 3.30: Level II Quality Controls – Alexa

TOPIC-SPECIFIC SEARCHES

Sometimes search engines try to atone for not knowing what we want by creating a boxed search – a set of results packaged according to a specific archive or collection. Some are exclusive. Some are common. Some are pretty generic. The nice thing about topic searches is that they let us bypass the ocean and start our search projects in the lake. That means all our topic-driven search results share a common property:

> 1. Format (images, video, audio, maps)
>
> 2. Time frame (news stories, blogs)
>
> 3. Origin (wikis, educational / government sites)

Specialty collections can expedite our searches because topic-specific searches are predefined source groupings that create containable buckets of content. These groupings limit the outcome to subjects covered within that collection — for instance, recipes on cooking sites, or federal policies within a collection of government agencies and bureaus.

What are some additional factors that would determine our success or satisfaction by running a topic-specific search?

For starters, anyone who uses syntax in a broad Google search knows that those settings fall apart when the same query is run in Google Images or Google Videos. That speaks to the pivotal role that semantics and pointers play in the smaller and less structured collections of topic-specific searches. We can constrain our searches to the lake of telephone listings:

rphonebook:johnson 207

That means all the residential phone records for one of the more common surnames in the State of Maine.[10]

Another example is to take a simple term like 'investigator' and invoke it in Yahoo's lake of subject directories:

FIGURE 3.31: Level II Quality Controls –Topic-specific Searches

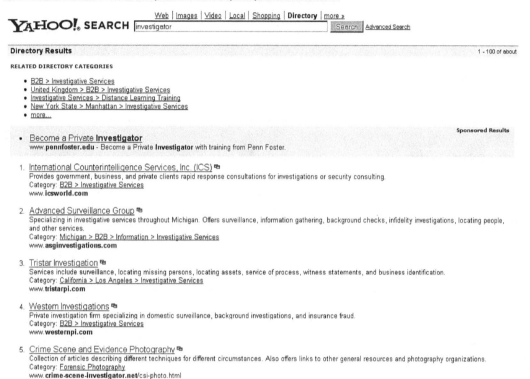

We're seeing two levels emerge here. The macro lens of related directory categories shows us the categorical buckets that our search term falls into. The micro view below is the routine set of search hits with one key distinction. The search rankings are not delivered through the advertising of keyword matches as with general web or ocean searches. Instead the rankings are determined by the strength of association between each website and its stature within the topic it's grouped in.

As we considered at the beginning of this section, so we remain the ultimate regulators. It's true. But there's still a place for government-sponsored quality control on the web. The most reliable quality check for source content remains the .gov domain for ensuring that the content of all DotGov sites is produced by the auspices of the U.S. Federal and State governments. We'll be re-introducing government-sponsored databases when we assess the Deep Web in the next section of **Unit Three**.

Finally, consider public records when reviewing Level II quality control options. Rather than subscription-supported, government information is tax supported and therefore needs to clear a much higher threshold on its accuracy and completeness than the lax standards governing private sources of information. This is not to suggest that governments always tell the truth or what we need to know. But it does mean that we still have a right to both. Something no one rightfully expects when searching cost-free information with an unlimited data plan.

FIGURE 3.32: Level II Quality Controls – Government Statistics

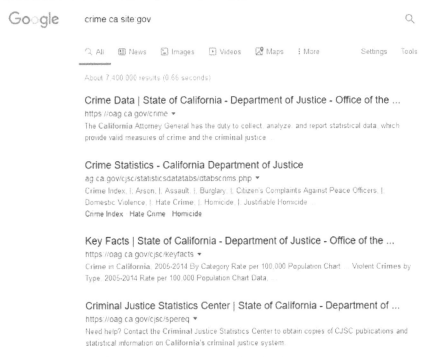

This is a selective ocean skimming that the site:gov syntax affords us as we pursue factual evidence for crime patterns both statewide and in unspecified California cities.

LEVEL II QUANTITY CONTROLS: SEARCH METRICS

So we choose our terms carefully and we try out a bunch of advanced tools to help refine our search results and we still produce thousands of sites that are probably more misses than hits. Does it really matter that our hit counts add up to 12,000 than 4 million? After all we're never going to open visit them all, let alone go beyond the first 1-2 screens to even guess whether it's worth continuing through on our expedition or whether it's time to regroup, right?

Well, believe it or not ... it does!

Quantifying hit counts allows us to exercise an overlooked evaluation tool that sits alongside quality control. Unlike site analysis or page scanning where one has to assess websites on a case-by-case basis, the high-level filtering afforded by quantity controls is critical to the success of our mission.

Ratio of Key Indicators

How do we manage the anticipated overload of search results from broadly-worded queries? The size of our search results can be just as important to your research as the content of any web page within those returns. Key ratios are important tests of hit counts that help investigators to...

- Budget their time

- Reformulate their queries

- Consider the popularity or visibility of particular issues and events

Key ratios are especially helpful for determining our proximity to an answer. This is when a realistic search goal means getting to the right person – not to the most relevant article or popular website. For finding people, key ratios...

- Determine the accuracy of hitting fact-based search targets such as specific individuals, event details, or groupings

- Rationalize the expense of follow-on work such as ordering individual background checks based upon the accuracy of the IDs provided

How many hits are too many hits? There are two ways to determine this. The *Sniff Test* measures how close we are to exact matches, such as making a positive ID on a particular person. The other way is a signal-to-noise ratio – a comparison of useful to useless results addressing the broader dimensions of topic or opinion-based searches.

Sniff Test

There is certainly one question that Google is not likely to answer any time soon. That's the reason for ballooning or declining hit counts. That's a test we can't rule out in the hot pursuit of the right individual, event, or topic we're targeting. Remember, it's the fact-based searches you are trying to prove or disprove. In the opinion searches, we are out to validate or invalidate where conclusions usually take longer to form. Hence, it's the tendency of higher counts to be less conclusive.

FIGURE 3.33: Hit Counts as Query Formation Indicators

Hit Counts	Modification
+50,000	Introduce syntax restrictions to limit your results to specific site addresses, page titles, or file formats
<50,000	Consider placing keywords in quotes
<10,000	Try expanding the number of search terms – introduce new keyword(s) to reinforce productive associations such as a group of relevant area codes to the person's residence and/or job titles and employment record

Now what are we getting back?

Are the results within our targeted area codes, state of residence, or even town or city? Can other nouns be added to the mix such as former employers, former colleges attended, mother's maiden name? What's the probability of a direct match? If not direct, what are the chances now that we've found some *homies* from the *hood*? Failing that, how about some potential colleagues within their social circles?

Signal-to-Noise Ratio

If we're looking more broadly at a topical search, the actual size of our counts matters less than the quality of the hits you're receiving in the first returns of your search results. What is the proportion of click-worthy sites (sites worth visiting) to dubious results? When sampling the first 30 records, first make sure they are unique pages. Single sites will often spawn multiple results. What should be our signal-to-noise ratio? Any result where at least half the results are click-worthy is a productive outcome.

FIGURE 3.34: Signal-to-Noise Metrics

Ratio	Click-worthy
33-50%	10-15 pages – above average
15-33%	5-10 pages – average
< 15%	Fewer than 5 pages – low

So in our first pass, how many of those first 30 records are worth a second look?

One way to separate signal from noise is to question their novelty. How many of these pages may tell us something useful we didn't already know? Another consideration is about the placement of our search terms. Do we see an abundance of highlighting in a majority of our page titles and summaries? Is this what we expected? Are we familiar with some of the recurring terms that are not highlighted?

LEVEL III QUALITY CONTROLS: PAGE SCANNING

So we've finally gotten to the light at the end of the bottom of the pile. We've tightened our control knobs. We've tweaked our site roots and content weights. We might not hold absolute mastery over every lever and metric. But we do know this. We're going in for the kill. Yes, we're convinced one search result or more are click worthy. We are now proceeding to Level III and there's no turning back. We are opening the links on our results lists.

Analyzing Page Scans

As we've seen in Levels I and II, we must monitor the query results for both quality and quantity. The tools and criteria vary depending on our site selection methods. Generally, the deeper we go, the greater our time commitment.

Now that we've landed on the actual page, what can we grasp immediately to know whether we're just passing through or here to stay? When making that determination, consider how much weight and credibility to give to individual information providers: Specifically, their motivations for sharing the details they select and opinions they provide.

FIGURE 3.35: Level III Quality Controls – Page Scans

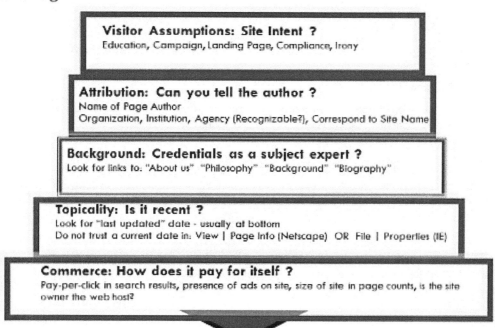

Page Scanning

Visitor Assumptions: Site Intent ?
Education, Campaign, Landing Page, Compliance, Irony

Attribution: Can you tell the author ?
Name of Page Author
Organization, Institution, Agency (Recognizable?), Correspond to Site Name

Background: Credentials as a subject expert ?
Look for links to: "About us" "Philosophy" "Background" "Biography"

Topicality: Is it recent ?
Look for "last updated" date - usually at bottom
Do not trust a current date in: View | Page Info (Netscape) OR File | Properties (IE)

Commerce: How does it pay for itself ?
Pay-per-click in search results, presence of ads on site, size of site in page counts, is the site owner the web host?

The Big Challenge:

Most Searchers Can't Process the Pages They Visit

Visitor Assumptions

What is the site intent? Why is it there? What calls to action does it implore to you, the visitor: education, marketing campaign, public issues and policies, landing page (shopping), regulatory compliance, humor (irony)?

Attribution

Can we tell who the author is? This is easier concluded with individuals than groups. Be wary of individuals who hide behind the mantle of representing an entire organizational structure as a means to inflate their own stature.

One simple credibility builder is the posting of a physical address and alternative means to make direct contact with the information provider – not just the site administrator who may have no control or interest in the content of the site itself. What kinds of associations are formed by the sites that link back to this one? Do we recognize these other sources and are they credible? Are the links reciprocal or are they unbalanced – either more linking to or from this site? Are there typos and broken links? These administrative details call a site's credibility into immediate question – regardless of how high the quality of its content.

Background

Does the provider offer credentials as a subject expert?

From a broader perspective what separates this information provider from related sites? We begin with links to some commonly used site conventions:

'About us' | 'Philosophy' | 'Background' | 'Biography' (pointers)

Are there experts on the team? Does the site present an assembly of their talents and contributions as a collective whole? How well do individual credentials serve the organizational mission or a company's competitive edge and key differentiators?

Topicality

How recently posted is the content on the site? Is it delivered through third parties or does it originate from this one? Is original content offered through alternative delivery such as RSS feeds? Monitor changes on pages and frequency of changes (profusion) – good for blogs and social media pages.

Is a pay-per-click program present on the site such as Google's AdWords? Will the acceptance of advertising influence the views they express. Will all the ads presented work in the site owner's favor or against, or some of the ads clearly irrelevant to the topics they cover?

Look for 'last updated' date - usually at bottom. The 'last updated' script automatically resets the displayed date on a web page each time the html source document is modified in any way – even if that update is based on pure automation like the refresh of an RSS feed. People assign more credibility to sites showing they have been recently updated or reviewed. Do not trust a current date in:

View | Page Info (Firefox), Chrome, or File | Properties IE ("Internet Explorer").

The lights may be on. But no one's home.

Now that we've tunneled down from our search binoculars to our page-scanning microscopes, it's time to focus outward. From the *what* to the *where* factors are what influence the content we're assessing before it ever reaches the quality control stage.

SECTION 3.4: | Managing Project Resources —

How Should We Think About Research Costs?

Before "we had privacy from obscurity," says David Ardia, fellow at the Berkman Klein Center for Internet & Society, and the director and founder of the Digital Media Law Project:

> *"Now, almost everything worth knowing about anyone is online."* **(Milliard, 2010)**[11]

Has that assertion lost its revelatory shine? The distinction between *always being on* and have such status apply to one's virtual rather than social life is long past the transition period.

It's important to note that the public side of resources here is the traditional view of milestones and legal histories such as...

- Births / Vaccinations,
- Mortgages / Deeds,
- Marriages / Divorces, and
- Criminal trespasses.

It does not reflect the personal details found in our browser plug-ins, downloads, email records, streaming patterns, and all transactions forming a digital identity that's concealed from us by its creators. That is an aspect of web investigations left to computer forensics experts, the courts, consumer advocates, and the legalese buried in the user agreements of the social and search giants that sell our personal data.

We will cover the following cost-related components of project resources:

1. Public and private records

2. The visible and invisible web

3. Free or fee (subscription) services

4. Consistent guidelines for searching

What's Public?

There is a big distinction in the availability, abundance, and legal standing of personal and impersonal information. Personal information has been held traditionally in confidence by the party being described. However, all that is changing with the increase in electronic records, the ease of wireless communications, and loopholes that invite infringements of our privacy. More often, the invitation to acquire personal information is not waiting on legal rulings or even questionable judgment. It's simply a matter of price.

As I promised before we started along the knowledge continuum, all of our discussions rest on this assumption: There are no additional surcharges or subscription fees involved in accessing, analyzing, or presenting the resources tackled in this book. Where do we draw the line? With so many personal details for sale by credit bureaus and information brokers, what rules do we follow to determine...

- What's available to us at the asking price of cost free?
- Also, what would we expect to find if we did pay a premium?

On the second point, we should reasonably assume that our clients have some experience in paying out-of-pocket for public records. The limitations of what they found prompts them to go the additional step. They come to us. In such cases, how do we demonstrate...

- The value we add as domain experts?
- The costs we've either reduced or sidestepped for our customers in that effort?

Here's our working definition: When a site or a page is *above the radar*, some type of documentation exists. Let's go back to the quality control section we've just concluded.Let's consider the likelihood that some record or web-based artifact exists before we commit to its capture. How do we determine if...

- It's public, and
- It's in a useful form.

We'll refer to this boundary between public and private as 'the radar.'

Being *above radar* means:

1. The visible web (what lives in the indexes of search engines) and not the deep or invisible web (more on that later)
2. Contact and biographic details but not hacking into subscription databases or password protected account details, encrypted messages, GPS-based travel settings, browser histories, etc.
3. Public records available online but not courthouse proceedings available through a court-order

Defining the Radar

It's difficult to overstate the slippery nature of what passes between public and private on the web. It cuts both ways. More records go online every day while other repositories can be pulled offline without warning or fanfare. Funding sources dry up for government sites. Business models fail in commercial ventures. Pilot projects get pulled — often through lack of revenue potential more than lack of use or interest. Also, there is nothing static about the kinds of information we wish to post about ourselves. Partly that's because social networks can increase the ease and distribution of experiences shared virtually. The other reason is us. A breach or compromising episode with social media may chasten our embrace of it. Again, it cuts both ways.

Another tool for sharpening our digital radar screens is to think about project sources in terms of content groupings. Some are easier to access than others. Some are more evolving and fluid. Some may require us to pay an access fee, and there's no getting around it. These personal effects include:

1. Social networks

2. Medical and driving records

3. Births, marriages, deaths

4. Career / employment histories

5. Personal assets

6. Credit histories

7. Transactions[12]

Now let's plot these project source groupings on our radar screen. The center line that runs through the radar perimeter is the surface between what we may expect to be public (above) and private:

FIGURE 3.36: The Great and Sometimes Blurry Divide Between Above and Below Radar

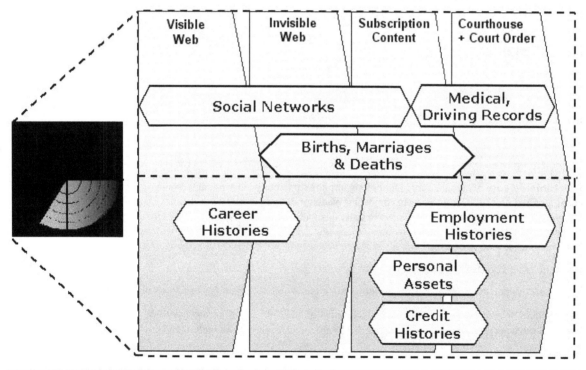

This diagram defines the above and below radar project sources through the availability of typically fee-based content in the pre-Smart phone era. Not surprisingly, the radar has and will continue to trend in the online direction of the visible web.

One way to put some of these concepts to the test is to enlist them in the number one investigative pursuit: Finding people — the world's oldest information profession.

PEOPLE FINDERS

So we're back at the tail-end of those quality controls. Those are the indications we should float on the ocean surface or dive down for a deeper exploration. Nowhere is this method put to a greater test than deciding whether the John W. Doe we're looked for is *the* John W. Doe.

There's the temptation to let go of the search page for the confirming rush that a person we've spotted in the highlighted keyword summaries is *the* person we've been targeting. Bullseye! Despite all the noise and common surnames, home towns, and pastimes held by our search target and throngs of imposters, we've nailed it down. It's not just a click-through worth tagging. It's a piece to the larger picture we're puzzling through in our search logs.

All too often that click-through is a proprietary database. It's disheartening to spend money in advance for details that may be useless to an investigation. But it's no less discouraging to stop in the same tracks as novice searchers who reach the same place through a garden variety Google search.

When someone offers public records, most times they are providing the range of background material we can pull on non-celebrities. That's right. Ordinary folks like you and me, matched to...

- Vital data: birth, marriage, death

- Education and certifications

- Religion and ethnicity

- Addresses and next of kin

- Employment and professional affiliations

- Real property ownership and liens

- Credit and payment histories

That's the checklist.

As long as there's compromising information, there will be traffickers to broker it. So here's what I think.

Put away the credit card. There are many side doors for entering into the same body of knowledge. While it helps to document a bad debt, or an unsettled score, the more compelling evidence doesn't come from a database but from the firsthand experience of those connected to the person we're searching. In these cases, searching is no more a means to an end as the discovery of a bad debt or a youthful indiscretion. We're searching for the sake of conversing: To establish a dialog or more formally conduct what used to be called *primary research* by engaging our networks directly.

Here are two important lessons on free resources to track down people:

1. They're best used on the front-end to narrow down our choices and document false positives beforehand.

2. The amount of diligence we apply needs to be factored into the terms of our research services. Just because a resource is public doesn't mean that the knowledge for how to use it is broadly understood or shared.

As we've seen with subject directories and cluster engines, the best interfaces can generate that periphery around a crime. The social circle surrounding the case. It's especially useful when we pool together our leads first. Then we search them as individuals on search engines that are dedicated to personal identities.

Sites such as Pipl and 123people sprung up in the mid-2000s[13]. Then the field became overrun with fee-based personal record brokers. These days, the number of social media profiles far eclipses the reach of any third-party broker. It's big search and social media who hold the master key to our personal effects, cross-referencing them with our demographics, travel patterns, and virtual identities. The personal lives of Facebook members are within the prying eyes of the faceless.

PURSUING EXECUTIVES

""There's only one thing worse than being talked about, and that is not being talked about."

– Oscar Wilde

Before social media began in earnest, there was a common rally cry for which individuals were fair game to target and track on the web. Celebrities weren't counted. (If they're not tracked, they're not *celebrated*). Business leaders on the other hand, are usually more comfortable having the limelight shine on their stock splits, shrewd acquisitions, and gravity-defying earnings. By and large, the corporate executives of publicly-traded companies remain ripe for picking. No undercover required for sourcing the personal backgrounds, perks, inner circles and sanctums of the upper echelon. It could be bonuses, stock options, real estate holdings, yachts, or Lear Jets. Space tourism to follow!

Personal property is an important validation tool for corporate researchers in fundraising operations. They support development officers needing to break the ice with well-heeled, potential donors. Real estate is one part of that pursuit. Many realty sites have popped up that approximate the housing and property values of exclusive neighborhoods where executives may own one or several upscale homes. Other personal assets may include private yachts, planes and other luxury transportation items that include some form of public registration.

Board affiliation sites track the executive's professional network beyond their own corporate borders. Donor status on political campaigns and alumni connections are other options for expanding the executive's networking profile.

Finally, there are numerous subscription-based sources for tracing corporate rumors and scandals to internally generated memorandums and email. But remember, however *premium* these sites claim to be, your fee pays admission to documents now combed over by anyone accessing the same password protected database. These sources while fee-based are by no means exclusive. Nor is their data always accurate and up-to-date.

Free Versus Fee – When to Use What

When is it better to use subscription or fee-based information sources than what is available free of charge via the web. We broached this idea earlier in this unit under Site Selection with the observation that conventional investigations tend to require chronological accuracy. That means a sequencing of discoveries that match the unfolding of the events they're based on. This is elusive on the web where sources disappear and time stamps can be misleading.

Another major improvement to our research is that we are instantly searching a well-stocked pond rather than an uncharted lake or ocean. That means sources are traceable. Credibility is resting on the good name of the publisher, at least when they're acting in the dual role of distributor. It's also fairly easy to discern the communities where the information we find has been circulating.

Speaking of circulation, what are some new frontiers that we can sway to our advantage as investigators? For starters, we can now put our fingers on the collective pulse of public opinion in ways that the best-financed polling operation could never have delivered through phone interviews or mall intercepts. Put another way, why is public awareness best addressed in a common web search? The answer lies in the radar devised in the following Google Trends interface:

FIGURE 3.37: The Powerful Pulse-taking Abilities of Google Trends

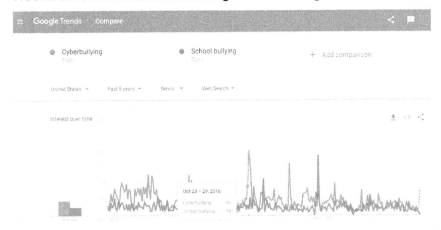

Here's a five year comparison between virtual and school yard bullying. Note the cyber-bullying spike in the home stretch of the 2016 election. These frequencies are restricted to queries.[14]

FIGURE 3.38: Correlating a Topic to Catalyst Events

	Related topics	Rising ▼ ± <> ⩽		Related queries	Rising ▼ ± <> ⩽
1	Ebola virus disease - Disease	+2%%	1	breast cancer prevention week	+2,900%
2	Alzheimer's Association - Non-profit association	+10%	2	when is breast cancer prevention week	+1,600%
3	Oseltamivir - Medication	+20%	3	how to prevent ebola	+1,200%
4	Alzheimer's disease - Disease	+20%	4	positive prevention plus	+25%
5	Pre-exposure prophylaxis - Topic	+15%	5	how to prevent dry drowning	+35%
	Showing 1-5 of 13 topics >			Showing 1-5 of 25 queries >	

FIGURE 3.39: Comparing a Topic (Preventative Healthcare) to a Drug Type (Antibiotics)

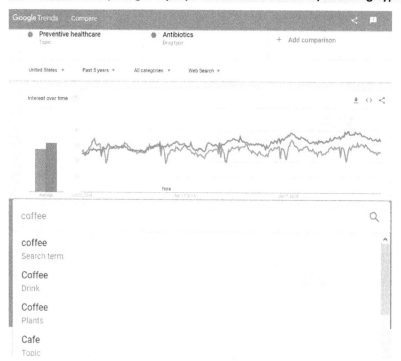

Above, a query on 'antibiotics' is identified by Google Trends as a medication. A selection table [LEFT] displays its classification codes in support of more accurate comparisons and contexts.

Another common challenge and opportunity for web investigators speaks to that gnawing question about fee-based public records. Are all public records available only through private vendors?

Absolutely not.

Resources from genealogists like Stephen P. Morse make it possible to confirm addresses and phone numbers otherwise commanding the surrender of our credit cards through brokers:

FIGURE 3.40: A Read-out from the Birthday Finder Application
(written by Stephen P. Morse)

	Name		Born	Address				Phone
1	MITCHELL	BANCHIK		161 73RD ST	NEW YORK	NY	10023	(212) 579-4656
2	MITCHELL	BANCHIK		161 73RD ST	NEW YORK	NY	10023	(212) 799-1734
3	MITCHELL	BANCHIK		161 73RD ST	NEW YORK	NY	10023	(212) 579-4656
4	MITCHELL	BANCHIK		161 73RD ST	NEW YORK	NY	10023	(212) 799-1734
5	MITCHELL	BANCHIK		300 76TH ST	NEW YORK	NY	10021	
6	MITCHELL	BANCHIK		161 73RD ST	NEW YORK	NY	10023	(212) 579-4656
7	MITCHELL	BANCHIK		161 73RD ST	NEW YORK	NY	10023	(212) 799-1734
8	MITCHELL	BANCHIK		161 73RD ST	NEW YORK	NY	10023	(212) 579-4656
9	MITCHELL	BANCHIK		161 73RD ST	NEW YORK	NY	10023	(212) 799-1734
10	MITCHELL	BANCHIK		300 76TH ST	NEW YORK	NY	10021	
11	MITCHELL	BANCHIK		161 73RD ST	NEW YORK	NY	10023	(212) 579-4656
12	MITCHELL	BANCHIK		161 73RD ST	NEW YORK	NY	10023	(212) 799-1734
13	MITCHELL	BANCHIK		161 73RD ST	NEW YORK	NY	10023	(212) 579-4656
14	MITCHELL	BANCHIK		161 73RD ST	NEW YORK	NY	10023	(212) 799-1734
15	MITCHELL	BANCHIK		300 76TH ST	NEW YORK	NY	10021	

15 matches found

These are public records gleaned from published directories and include wire line phone numbers and residential addresses. Mr. Morse has developed a mashup – a search interface that crawls different people finder databases on the web, allowing users to access those details for research purposes, a.k.a. free.

Perhaps the greatest opportunity for above radar people searches is to focus the bigger people finder picture on social networks. Again, the relative openness of the web enables a more complete picture – if not always a clear one. We'll need a positive ID before we can glean an individual's connection to these other aspects of a social identity: Communities, employers, professional affiliates and authored works.

Figure 3.41 details when it's more productive to use openly accessible or premium sources. As we can see, the more concrete the answers called for by your project, the likelier that definitive or subscription sources will be called on. Conversely, the more socially connected our research, the likelier we'll call on free sources that measure and reflect popular opinion or a broader public awareness.

FIGURE 3.41: The Checklist of What's Best Answered on a Free and Fee Basis

	Web (free)	Premium (fee)
Perception	X	
Public Records		X
Motivation	X	
Publication Archive		X
Legal Documents		X
Social Network	X	
Source Distribution		X

THE VISIBLE AND INVISIBLE WEB

Search engines perform an amazing service. They trawl the vast expanse of the virtual world, mapping for us an ocean full of information that can appear as incalculable and infinite as the universe itself. And they do it not in days or weeks but in milliseconds.

Yet if truth be told, this engineering feat is not the whole truth. It brings its own shortcuts and distortions. This includes lots of below-the-surface depth the never makes it into the search index. That's because there are many places that are either too detailed to document or off-limits to commercial search engines.

Period.

Remember that old adage that we humans only utilize a scant portion of our brain capacity? The same analogy might well serve the 3%-5% of the web which surfaces in Google[15]. Basically, there's a lot of *stuff* that search engines can't or won't search. These include:

1. Dynamically generated pages (weather, news, job postings, market prices, travel schedules...)

2. Web accessible or common theme databases that require information be typed in (laws, dictionaries, directory lists...)

3. Sites that require password or logins to access

4. Commercial resources with domain or IP limitations

5. Intranets

If we consider the limited scope of what a search tool can index, it would be appropriate to refer to Google or Bing as the *visible* or *shallow* web. The recesses of the Internet resistant to being indexed are alternatively called the *invisible* or *the deep web*. Either way, the stuff below the surface might be a worthwhile place for an investigator to scope out.

Here's what we might find in the deeper recesses of the web:

1. It is narrower in scope with greater depth of documentation than more conventional sites.

2. OLP-wise, it's full of lakes. Over half its pages derive from databases, primarily from government-maintained archives like U.S. National Oceanic and Atmospheric Administration, NASA, the Patent and Trademark Office and the Securities and Exchange Commission's EDGAR search system.[16]

3. Not surprisingly, its content is highly relevant to domain and subject matter experts.

4. Fully 90% of its content is publicly accessible information — not subject to access fees or subscriptions.[17]

More than half its content resides in topic-specific databases. This is where researchers can use the deep web to drill down into the matching patterns formed by overlapping facts and document properties contained in database records. If this sounds like that Ocean-Lake-Pond routine again that's good. Just remember the deep web doesn't mean we're in too deep when it takes us to the correct pond for checking in on the specifics of our case.

In sum, remember to take the deep web plunge when...

■ Standard search engines aren't working

■ We need data or statistics (from one source addressing one topic)

■ We need high quality or authoritative results

■ Timeliness is overruled by the need to get our facts straight through validation and confirmation

■ We either know the subject area well or have confidence we'll find what we're seeking

■ We are looking for collections (images, sounds, manuscripts, birth/death records, etc.)

FIGURE 3.42 Why Two Internets? Defining the Deep Web

Searching the web =
    dragging a net across the ocean surface.

- Engines create indexes by crawling "surface" Web

- Discovery requires pages to be static and linked

- Can't retrieve searchable databases that only appears dynamically in responding

DEEP WEB GATEWAYS: GETTING FROM OCEANS TO LAKES

Throughout **Unit Three** we've considered some of the complicated syntax to get from a commercial search engine like Google (ocean) down to a searchable database (pond). It's in the pond where we can actually yield specific facts, historic records, and contact information we typically need in searching reference sources in support of virtual investigations.

In our OLP examples, we first prove the existence of an index or an archive on the shallow web. First, we come up with a list of searchable directories and indexes. Next, we use syntax or go to the site directly. We view the site map to confirm that databases, statistics, or other reference materials mentioned. Finally we fish. We use the site's internal search tool and do the trawling that only investigators, not algorithms can provide.

There is a more direct approach than relying on convoluted text strings and metadata fields. There are specialty search engines designed to capture more scholarly-inclined sources and archives. They offer publicly accessible databases in domains welcoming to researchers.

That said, a simple page design can conceal lots of potentially useful details. Remember our discussion about visualization engines in **Unit Two**? The results, though attractive, don't impart a sense of how much more is left to cover once we consume the visuals.

It's easier to tell a search engine by its advertising than by its *cover*, meaning design elements. The top level view of the deeper story can be misleading. That's the flip-side of the analogy: The lack of depth under the visualization scheme.

FIGURE 3.43: Getting from an Ocean to a Pond Through a Deep Web Search Engine

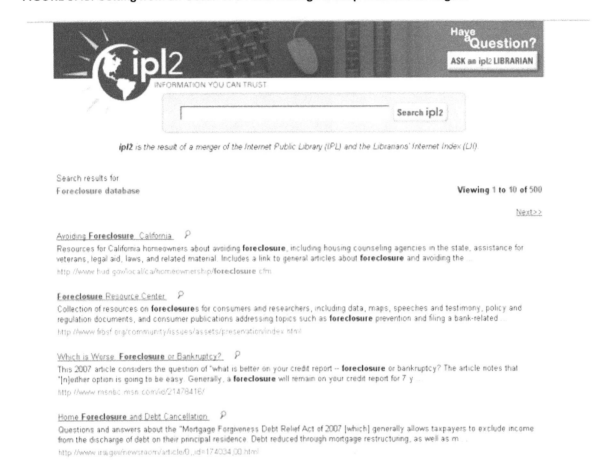

It's interesting to note that resources billing themselves as deep web searches are really metasearch engines. They don't index websites. They search the indexes. And like its source, only a scant amount of information is actually indexed. That's another reason that the Internet Ocean is a *shallow* one. Deep web sources like databases (Internet ponds) cannot be stored within these memory limits.

That's the most important takeaway from the humbling limits of search engines: They perform the illusion of searching the ocean when at best they are searching a few inches below the surface. If we want access to the sites that don't float to the Google surface, it's a deeper web where we can find much higher value information. The trade-off is that we know where we're going. We can't scale the deep web like we can search the ocean surface. By definition, we're searching pond-by-pond. It is exacting and often painstaking work. But well worth the effort when landing the gold nugget that closes the books on our case.

The dynamic nature of the web as a publishing platform is a more subtle but notable limitation of search engines. Searching the web can be like dragging a net across the ocean surface: Search engines create indexes by *skimming* the *surface* web. For a page to be discovered, it must be static and linked. We cannot retrieve searchable databases that only appear dynamically in responding to queries. Database records cannot be bookmarked or tagged. Remember: Each invisible web source is an index. That index become part of its cached record on the search engine site – even if a particular page or record is altered or removed.

Visualizing the Invisible

Contrary to self-serving motives, not everyone wants more traffic to their websites and social profiles. Sometimes sites are built to satisfy a legal or regulatory order. Sometimes a small group hosts discussions for a select group of participants. Sometimes a body of knowledge is indexed. It's stored by domain experts in the same way that scribes and archivists copied and preserved ancient texts. This goes on regardless of whatever the appeal may be to a wider audience. So we've cracked open the door of the deep web. We have these basic ideas about what it contains that the commercial search engines can't or won't index:

1. Thousands of specialized searchable databases that require us to enter information into their own search structure (laws, dictionaries, directory lists...)

2. Sites that require a password or login

3. Commercial resources with domain or IP limitations

FIGURE 3.44 Databases as Search Results on the Deep Web

The invisible web is a rich combination of databases, new or non-linked text files, other file types, etc. Many of these are accessible through a front-end or specially designed search programs. Here a deep web search like Complete Planet offers databases as search results. *This site has since been decommissioned.*

Searching Out Loud: Giving Voice to Independent Investigations | Marc Solomon

Premium Services

Premium or fee-based subscription services are an effective way to close the gap between the shortcomings of the free web or public domain and the objectives of your investigation.

Premium services date back to the 1970s when vendors such as LEXIS/NEXIS, Dow Jones News Retrieval, and DIALOG became online access providers to commercial publications, financial reports, and specialized government and scientific databases. These sources were sourced and searched almost exclusively by librarians and information professionals. Small wonder the documentation they contain is consistent and thorough in how it's gathered and classified.

These premium information services enable researchers to do the impossible on the web: Trace their findings to specific information providers. There is little doubt who the information provider is when an investigator takes direct testimony or interviews eyewitnesses. Collecting evidence off the web is a bigger challenge.

Many are not up to this challenge. They focus on the evidence-gathering to the exclusion of where they're getting it from. As we've seen, this carries is a potentially grave risk to any investigation given the unregulated state of the web's content suppliers.

In addition to the added trust of traceable sources, premium services are effective tools for connecting keywords to organized topics. Their structure makes it possible to sort information chronologically. That helps us verify a proper sequence of events in our investigations. Figure 3.45 contains some of the key distinctions in favor of using premium sources in our investigation.

FIGURE 3.45: Fee Services: Defining Added Benefits

Benefit	Feature
Concept of "added value"	Large archive Repeated access Complex concepts
Concept of source organization	Higher selectivity Better bundling
Syntax used in large subscription-based collections	More exacting, literal – 1-2 word queries are often useless
Sites	www.factiva.com www.highbeam.com infotrac.galegroup.com

So what are the trade-offs of using premium services? The downsides are pretty simple:

1. Because they are not published by the information providers.

2. They are not up-to-date.

3. They are not free.

Dated Information:

It's ironic. But in the days before the web premium services were disparaged as *secondary sources.* The inference is that secondary research is second-hand, old or dated. The premise here is that we can't rely on their data. There's nothing new about the tendency for history taking a backseat to immediacy. But it's also a timeless reality that background and context reveals everything about a campaign, market, or management practice. What worked? What was was scrapped? Which lessons bear repeating? Which decisions still haunt those who made them?

Exclusive Sources:

Going exclusively with premium services introduces another risk to our search projects. Think of subscription-based collections as the walled-in gardens of the information forest. They are seeded, weeded, and watered by professional groundskeepers (database catalogers and taxonomists). However, that control level only extends to a postage stamp-sized footprint of cultivated, higher quality information. The overwhelming world beyond its borders carries an entire set of actions and outcomes that will never grow within the delicate confines of a premium database.

REVISITING SOURCE FLUENCY

Earlier in this unit we introduced the concept of source fluency: The practice of building up our source knowledge as an independent researcher. In this final section of **Unit Three**, a reintroduction is in order as a project resource in its own right.

Knowledge is no longer books and periodicals: it is content and substance.

In the post-Web Wide World, a source is still a source. But *how* one finds the source is an open invitation to better and varied sources. In this new environment, *book smart* is supplanted by navigational whim. Route takes precedence over destination. A fixed set of sources is pure baggage. Collections are now the province of churches and museums – not Internet-based investigators.

Re-enter source fluency. As we've established source fluency is about knowing where to look for information without knowing what it is called. It means having the discipline and dexterity to determine both *how* and *where* to search.

Source fluency is the ability to know and develop where to look for information without needing to know what it is called its specific storage location. One commonly used and often ineffective process for cultivating fluency is bookmarking previously or potentially helpful sites for future recall. The problem with bookmarks is that they lose their utility over time. That's because they require us bookmarkers to recall the original reasons and places where we put them.

With source fluency, the emphasis is on the action we're trying to accomplish.Not the source, tool, or application that served us once and may yet again. This means that the resource will be there when we need it, regardless of the investigation, or our prior understanding of it.

Another important element of source fluency is that we can trace a topic to the best interest of the information provider on the subject. We're fluent in web sourcing without needing to know established authorities, back channels of gossip, or official keepers of records. That means we can reliably find credible and vested sources that cover subjects we'll need to familiarize and understand – if not master – in our research travels.

Information as a Verb

At first it may sound self-evident that source mastery boils down to how we assess them (quality controls) and where we going looking (site selection). But there is a temptation to hire the answer doctor. That's the source expert who never needs to ask an original question because they've committed every qualified information provider to memory. The myth of the answer doctor lives on even in this day and age of Twitter handles and instant analysts who fabricate their sites to look authoritative.

Here are a few ironclad tenets that come with the source fluency turf:

1. There is only one 'what' (the question we're addressing) but there are many 'hows' (sources).

2. Sources do not count unless you know how to pose the question.

3. The focus is not on the ever-shifting answers you need, but on fielding the right set of questions to find them.

4. Information devoid of its social, marketing and technical implications is meaningless.

So if source fluency is so superior to answer doctors, how do we put this new asset to work in our search projects?

Defining Credibility

Reputation colors information providers like shadows follow suspicions. One misleading headline and all subsequent reports are stained with a lurking suspicion that the news source has given a limited or self-selective base of facts around a breaking story. At least that was the role reputation played before the only barrier to conjecture and publication was the <send> key on our keyboards. Reputation still matters because gauging one is more elusive than ever.

To a generation raised on the web, the term 'credibility' may carry a different meaning. For instance, being credible may have less to do with being believed and more to do with ability to be influential because of their numerous connections or ample resources. It could also simply mean greater clout or personal stature:

> *"I don't know what your face looks like. [W]e're twitter beefing now. [I]t's gonna raise my credibility as a rapper so yeah. [b]eef."* **(Lynette, 2010)**[18]

At first, it may seem like a subtle distinction between taking someone seriously and taking someone at their word. But the differences and their consequences can be dramatic.

Let's say for instance that I'm a blogger who could use a few spare dollars. I allow Google to post what it deems to be relevant ads to my website. Well, this cuts in two opposing directions. On one hand, my blogging site might seem less credible because the ads may undermine the editorial style and substance of the blog. On the other hand, the site may appear more established and even a more authoritative source. That's because the Google ads lend institutional legitimacy to what is essentially a one-man band.

Regardless of how we define credibility, our common goal as researchers rests in one determination: What matters the most in the discussions inspired by our search targets? We can weigh what facts rise to the head of a debate. We can formulate how widespread those facts are distributed and how much agreement actually exists about them among the groups most likely to lead the charge or be impacted by the events in question. We can even pinpoint hypocrisies between what a well-known person says in settings of their choosing versus the actions they take. Actions taken assumes less guarded and often less favorable or riskier circumstances.

Later on in **Unit Four** we will introduce **Provider Source Conjugation**. This is a framework that helps us to see the social value of information. That means how we appear on the web and how this impacts how others perceive us. If we use the same framework on the people we search, we can also use it to assess source bias as well. That could mean distortions and character defamation, intended or unintentional – for instance, what facts get selected and which ones don't.

DISCERNING SOURCE SELF-INTEREST

The top of the source fluency list of priorities is getting to the question of self-preservation. That's right. Finding out why information providers share what we're sourcing. Motivation focuses on classifying sources in two ways:

> **1. Peer reviews** – Specifically the inherent strengths and weaknesses of provider types.

> **2. Packaging** – Understanding how providers bundle their content *before* we integrate it with our own findings to the client.

First let's address the question of provider peer groups.

What we've lost is not some track record or backlog of questionable decisions. It's the notion of a 'reliable source' for information. It's the separation between who's making the news and who's reporting it. Without that distinction it is difficult to isolate what others say about us from what we petition on our own behalf. And nowhere is this problem harder to contain than that critical group of observers from which all reputations are grounded, shaped, and most importantly ... believed:

> 1. Direct experience with the search target.

> 2. No vested interest in any status change to that target, (be it a lawsuit, a job offer, or a substantial and pending sale).

A profusion of newsmakers masquerading as information providers does little to clarify this question of self-interest. It's especially hard to find impartial judges who are firsthand witness to the character and reputation of the individuals and groups we're investigating.

Now, let's consider packaging.

The primary benefit of premium sources is that they eliminate the uncertainty of who the ultimate source is for the information we're receiving. It doesn't hurt that they also provide...

> ■ Better classifications

> ■ Chronological sorting, and

> ■ Mapping keywords to topics

We'll delver further into these benefits in the next section.

Think about all the searching we've done where we knew definitive authorities? Where we could even reference the underlying fact-base that supports our assertions? But because it's the web, there's no clear path from search results to the subject knowledge we've accrued through our experience.

It's frustrating at best to vet the specific interests or incentives behind any one provider. The web remains largely an unregulated resource of self-selecting information sources. In **Unit Four,** we'll explore new frameworks that can help make this expectation reasonable and objective possible.

The Hidden Value in Paying for Information

Premium services have a number of advantages over the public or free web. For starters when information is paid for that usually confers some immediate advantages over free web-based content:

1. **Editorial oversight** – Having actual humans minding the info store means we benefit from formal tagging structures called taxonomies. That guarantees we get something in a structured database that's so elusive on the web: The context of categorical boundaries. Categorization maps news articles to their topical value. Want more of the same? Just click on the topic that the piece falls under. How the information we're targeting is grouped by professional classifiers is a level of control commercial web searches can't offer because they have no commercial incentive to provide this.

2. **Legal boundaries** – The fact that a for-profit or peer-reviewed publication formally releases a series of articles on a periodic basis makes them an information publisher in the traditional sense. That means they are held up to the standards and safeguards inherent in the First Amendment, including constitutional protections against slander and other civil liberties. Proving the same on the unregulated web carries a much higher legal burden for would-be plaintiffs.

3. **Causes and effect** – Another overlooked benefit is the simple assertion that we have a confirmable source, and with that, the reasonable certainty of a specific audience they're intending to reach. Connecting that relationship as the backdrop to the articles we're assessing helps us to understand the unstated nature of news coverage: Mainly *why* certain stories are covered and how these stories are told. The other advantage of cause-and-effect is to exploit the chronology of publication dates. That makes it easier to source the sequential order of the events we're tracking. In a fee-based model, date ranges speak to publication dates, not crawler sessions for indexing web pages.

4. **Repeatable responses** – This sounds like a scientist who over thinks the problem of inconsistent search results. Actually, few findings are more compelling to an investigation (and the client we're working for) than their ability to repeat our research. That means coming up with the same evidence we're using to draw conclusions in our investigations. That level of validation is much easier to attain in a stable resource than the dynamic and slippery web.

Figures 3.46 and 3.47 serve as examples of those benefits and some situations where they're of highest value to our investigation.

FIGURE 3.46: Advantages of Premium or Fee-based Content

Advantage	Examples
Concept of "added value"	• Large archive • Repeated access • Complex concepts
Concept of source organization	• Higher selectivity • Better bundling
Syntax used in large subscription-based collections	• More exacting, literal • 1-2 word queries are often useless

Below, we see how a fee-based service retained by the University of Michigan classifies subjects according to keywords. This is similar to the kind of results we find with a robust subject directory. The primary difference here is that the results lead to abstracts or complete articles from magazines, journals, and newspapers.

FIGURE 3.47: Context Through the Categorical Boundaries of Fee-based Content

"missing children" investigation unsolved autis*	🔍 Search	Advanced

Subject	—
missing persons	303
criminal investigations	268
kidnapping	190
unsolved crimes	149
murders & murder attempts	143
law enforcement	119
children & youth	117
investigations	110
murder	73
families & family life	65

Above we see our search target as both organizational and topic-based classifications. A further breakdown of those topics cross-references the main subject against a myriad of related themes that factor into it.

THE COST OF FREE TOOLS

So it's nice to know actual dates of articles grouped into understandable categories. It's also reassuring to know they were placed there with the care and discretion of a human editor. But let's get real, you say. Even if we did have a budget and a more flexible deadline, none of that matters. It won't change the fact that the action falls outside these subscription-based news archives. It's happening as we speak. And just because we don't know the source doesn't mean it's any less relevant to our investigation.

I'm not here to fall on my credibility sword over confusing or poorly-documented information sources. But it is important to know and identify the nature of the beast. And the monster in question is not out to conceal truth or hide criminals so much as act in its own self-interest.

As Andrei Hagiu and Bruno Jullien write in "*Why Are Web Sites So Confusing,*" there is a fundamental conflict between the needs of web investigators and web advertisers. **(Hagel, Julien, 2009)**[19] They argue that gateways like Google have little incentive to help us become more efficient searchers. Hagiu and Julien say that the revenues generated by pay-per-click ads push the more useful search results off the first results page. The effect is what the authors call 'search diversion.' That means steering users to products that yield the highest margins for search vendors.

This bias towards generating revenues ahead of insights is not limited to the ranking of web sites. Since 2011, it includes the 'search suggest' patterns that complete the half-formed queries now in all Google searches. That means that we're not only being guided in the direction of the sponsored ads but even the search terms that are bid up in the auctioning of keywords through the Google AdWords program.

Institutional Credibility

Personal credibility is a quality we assign to a trusted confidante. Someone who knows us well enough, communicates in ways we understand, and knows their way around the issues they advise us on. Institutional credibility is different. Like person-to-person counsel, believing what organizations tell us probably means we've been steered correctly by them in the past. But it also means something a lot less personal is taking place – even impersonal in matters of dispensing advice.

The reputations of advice-giving groups like stock brokerages and law practices hinge on how far removed they are from the counsel they keep. The closer their fortunes align with the professionals they advise, the likelier they place their own interests ahead of their clients. Having a direct interest in the connections they broker is sometimes called double-dipping because the adviser is compensated twice – both by the client and their own referral networks. It is also a clear conflict of interest.

Credibility before the Web

In pre-digital days of fee-based content, it didn't take a rigorous methodology to determine credibility. It meant that if the bastions of business media and research had an insight to share on their pages then their big wheel subscribers had an edge over non-subscribers: Those *yokels* who turned to the local paper but not the Wall Street Journal, for instance.

Figure 3.48 shows what a *food chain* of credible information providers might have looked like in the mid-nineties at the advent of the World Wide Web:

**FIGURE 3.48: Traditional Publishers of Fee-based Content
(and Their Former Spheres of Influence)**

Who	What	Why	Cost
Investment Reports	Advice to investors and underwriting of future IPOs	1 hour lunch meetings with CEO, CFO	Fee
Major Business	Full 'take no prisoners' investigations, industry report cards	Large editorial staffs and readerships	Fee
Regional Business	Intimate reporting on changes in management, labor, infrastructure operations	Unfailing way to see intimate side of global competitors but local angle means having turf to protect	Free
Management Journals	Gurus, methods, and teachers	Business development tool for academics and management consultants	Free
Trade Publications	Distribution,sales, spending patterns, product evaluations, and launches	Trade sources geared towards managers have more credibility than those aimed at marketers. Put your faith in what customers experience, not what vendors promise	Fee
Newswires	Real-time updates with an emphasis on financial transactions	The most prolific intelligence sources and the least analytical	Free
Blogs and Newsletters	Real-time with analysis	Need for rapid opinion formation favors speculation over reliability	Free
Press Releases	Generated by the source it addresses	The antithesis of integrity. Self-serving by definition	Free

Nowadays there is little distinction between breaking news and analyzing what it all means. Instant analysis is a paradox of the 24/7 news cycle where a restless parade of events overwhelms the cyclical rituals once used for pattern-matching and perspective-gathering. So who is worth paying attention to? It was a simpler matter in the old days where information made no distinction between *fee* and *free*. Whoever drew the biggest audiences commanded the most authority. This is not that different from the social media definition of credibility: The more followers, the more worth following. Below is an illustration of that top-down framework in Figure 3.49 for assessing institutional credibility in bygone days.

FIGURE 3.49: The Pyramid of 20ᵗʰ Century Institutional Credibility

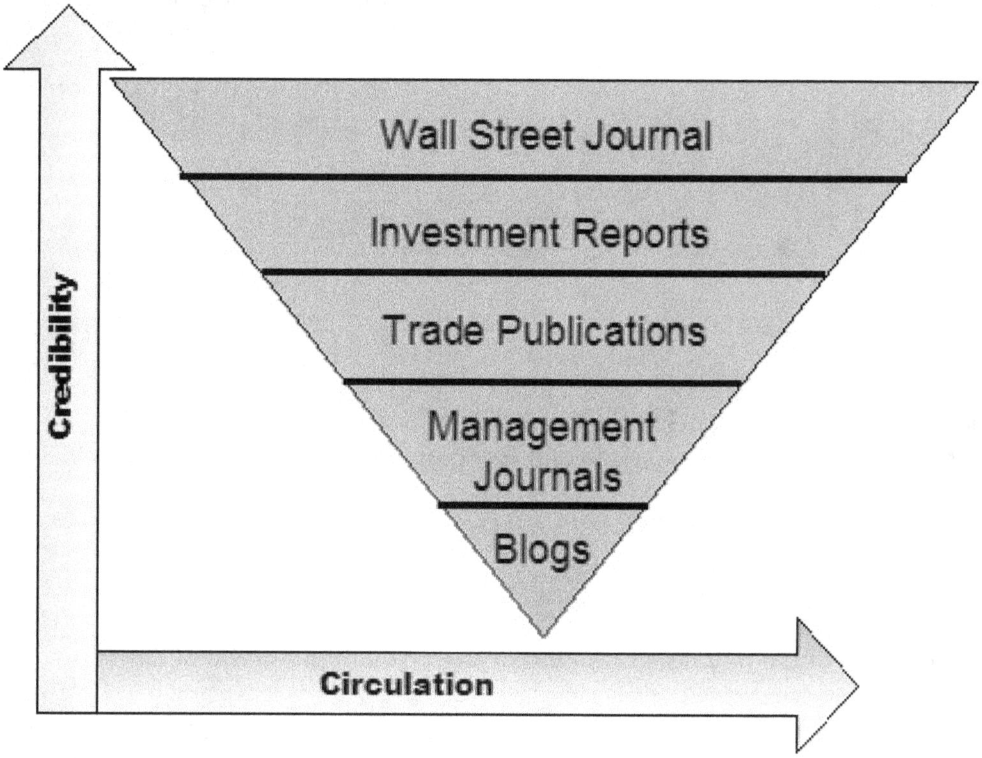

The wider the audience the higher an information provider's credibility as the above model from the fee-based era indicates That level of certainty has been obliterated by page ranks, reciprocal links, pay-per-click campaigns and the highly dubious business of quantifying influence in a web-based media environment.

UNIT THREE: Wrapping

How to Source Information That Instructs

Unit Three continued the discovery process modeled in the Knowledge Continuum. **Unit One** introduced the idea of organizing the discovery process through Search Planning Management. **Unit Two** centered on the vigorous tweaking needed to filter the noise from our search results. **Unit Three** focused on the frameworks used to address the motivations and priorities of providing web-based source content. We assessed the context, credibility, and cost factors associated with determining the merit of our references and quality of the information they produce. Once we understand how to plan, filter, and assess our research, we'll be poised to analyze and interpret our search results (**Unit Four**) into the core findings that we'll share with our clients (**Unit Five**).

[1] Jamais Cascio, "Get Smart," The Atlantic, July / August 2009

[2] Galen Stocking, Katerina Eva Matsa, "Using Google Trends data for research? Here are 6 questions to ask: First, what sort of research questions can Google data answer?" Medium, April 27, 2017)

[3] "What is the maximum size of an HTML file that Google will crawl through?" https://webmasters.stackexchange.com/questions/47233, April 12, 2013

[4] Barry Schwartz, "Google Crawl Limit Per Page Now Couple Hundred Megabytes," Search Engine Roundtable, August 3, 2017

[5] Patrick Stox, "20 of Google's limits you may not know exist," Search Engine Land, September 6, 2017

[6] The deep web is often confused for the dark web, a small subset that plays host to criminal activity, illegal transactions, and deviant behavior, i.e. sex trafficking, counterfeiting, pedaphilia, contract killing, etc.

[7] The Google Blog search application was discontinued in 2011.

[8] George Will,"Boredeom and the Cost of Constant Connection," Newsweek, August 14, 2010.

[9] This Amazon Alexa predates the robotic assistant by 20 years..

[10] Both the phonebook syntax and Google Videos were discontinued by Google in 2010 and 2011 respectively.

[11] Mike Milliard, "The World is Watching," The Boston Phoenix, September 23, 2010

[12] This is a pretty deep well and spans from purchase orders and phone logs to virtual sessions, payment patterns, and GPS coordinates (our physical whereabouts).

[13] 123people closed shop in 2014..

[14] A former version of the product compared keyword queries to press coverage of the same keyword-derived queries.

[15] J.J. Rosen, "The Internet You Can't Google," May 2, 2014, The Tennessean

[16] Jose Pagliery, "The Deep Web You Don't Know About," March 10, 2014, CNN Business

[17] Open Education Database, "The Ultimate Guide to the Invisible Web,"

https://oedb.org/ilibrarian/invisible-web/

[18] Tweet from Nikki Lynette, September 20, 2010

[19] Andrei Hagiu and Bruno Jullien, "Why Are Websites So Confusing," HBS Working Knowledge, October, 19, 2009

About the Author

Marc Solomon has been a knowledge architect, search manager, and competitive intelligence director in the acronym-laced world of strategic consulting (PwC, PRTM, FSG, and FIND/SVP) as well as tech services (BellSouth, Avid Technology, and Hyperion Solutions).

He currently works in the office of the CTO at The Hartford insurance company. He's presented on search, metadata, taxonomy, and Knowledge-ABLED practices through the Boston KM Forum, Enterprise Search Summit, Gilbane, and SIKM (Systems Integrators KM Leaders).

From 2005 to 2010 he was an adjunct professor in Boston University's Professional Investigation Program where he trained budding PIs on using the web to crack criminal cases, including instruction in digital media research and information literacy.

Mr. Solomon is a contributing columnist to several trade magazines on enterprise knowledge tools, practices and business cases including Searcher, Baseline, and KM World where he contributed a year-long "reality series" of SharePoint case deployment profiles. Solomon has addressed the realities of day-to-day content management as an expert blogger in the AIIM SharePoint Community. As a search expert and knowledge guru, he has decades of experience in teaching students how to become more information literate.

Most recently he launched an Open Source Intelligence (OSINT) program at the Montague Book Mill for mid-career professionals as founder of the Society for Useful Information, whose mission is to improve the quality of digital literacy and research practices throughout Western New England.

Solomon holds a BA in the History of Technology from Hampshire College and a Masters in Professional Studies from the Graduate School of Political Management at George Washington University. He lives with his wife Patty, Jaspurr the cat, and occasionally their three grown children in a home with no smart speakers and where no one searches in silence.

www.ingramcontent.com/pod-product-compliance
Lightning Source LLC
Chambersburg PA
CBHW082122070326
40690CB00049B/4108